I remember first studying the doctrine of sin  the number of Hebrew and Greek words for sin. But infinitely overtopping our sins is the merc God. Distinguished pastor-theologian Derek T thoughtful expressions of confessing our sins and of being refreshed and renewed by the ever-flowing streams of God's mercy. Such mercy, we know, comes at the cost of our Savior's obedience and blood. I often think how blessed I would have been to sit under the ministry of Dr. Thomas at First Presbyterian Church. I will gladly take this book as a consolation.

Stephen J. Nichols
President, Reformation Bible College, Sanford, Florida

Luke tells us that there is joy in heaven over one sinner who repents. This volume of confessions of sin and assurances of pardon will help us do just that: to enter into the paradoxical joy of repentance. These are beautiful prayers framed by Scripture, helping us: to pray with understanding and depth, to grasp the gravity of our sin, and to marvel at the wonder and joy of forgiveness. They will help every Christian, but they will certainly help those of us who have the privilege of leading our people in weekly confession of sin and will help churches as they use them.

Paul Levy
Minister, International Presbyterian Church, Ealing

When I first heard Derek Thomas preach thirty years ago, his prayers touched me as deeply as his sermons. They confronted my soul with the two great "immensities and infinities" of the Christian life: the overwhelming glory of God and the depth of my own sin. Too often, in our haste to get to the "real" work of prayer, we neglect confession. But through his example, and now with this book, Derek offers a needed reminder. Expect to be humbled, drawn closer to God, and brought to the Throne, where grace and mercy reign.

Neil C. Stewart
Senior Minister, First Presbyterian Church, Columbia, South Carolina

Foreword by Sinclair B. Ferguson

Approaching *the* Throne *of* God

Confessions of Sin & Assurances of Pardon

Derek W. H. Thomas

Afterword by Dale Ralph Davis

CHRISTIAN
FOCUS

Copyright © 2025, Derek W. H. Thomas

ISBN 978-1-5271-1199-8
Ebook ISBN: 978-1-5271-1286-5

Christian Focus Publications, Ltd
Geanies House, Fearn,
Ross-shire, IV20 1TW, Scotland
www.christianfocus.com

Cover and internal design by Daniel van Straaten

Printed by Bell & Bain, Glasgow

Edited by
William Grayson Lambert, Deborah Wells Thompson

With the assistance of Campbell Johnson Cathcart, Lanneau William Lambert, Jr., Marshall Braddoch Martin, Gordon Stowe Query, Ashtyn Outhous deBessonet

Special thanks to Sinclair B. Ferguson and Dale Ralph Davis

Contents

Foreword

Towards the end of his ministry, in a comment to Timothy, his closest colleague and friend, the apostle Paul refers to the heartbeat and goal of the ministry they had shared together. He writes: "The aim of our charge is love that issues from a pure heart and a good conscience and a sincere faith" (I Tim 1:5). The gifts of preaching and teaching, leading, and guiding are certainly important. But love is essential. Without it, no man should become a minister.

When Derek Thomas came to Columbia in 2011, he arrived with the reputation of being an outstanding preacher, an experienced pastor, and an esteemed seminary professor. But in all of these aspects of his ministry, he has made it his aim to love and to serve. And in doing so he has modelled some other words of Paul: "What we proclaim is not ourselves, but Jesus Christ as Lord, *with ourselves as your servants for Jesus' sake*" (II Cor 4:5).

Derek has expressed this servant love in many ways—in expounding Scripture, in teaching doctrine, in leading, in befriending, in encouraging, in challenging—and not least in praying. And this little book, which will be long treasured, is a special expression of that love.

Books of confessions of sin and assurance of pardon are widely available. But this one is unique. Its contents are an expression of a minister's special love and care for his own congregation, framing confessions and words of assurance designed to help one church family. For the only people Derek had in mind, over the closing years of his ministry as he penned these words, was First Presbyterian Church of Columbia, South Carolina. Indeed, as this book goes to press, and its contents now become widely available, he will have no knowledge of it until it is presented to him as his ministry draws to a close.

These prayers have been among the many love-gifts of Derek Thomas's ministry to the people he has supremely loved and with whom he has been bound in the same bundle of life.

As members of the congregation read them—perhaps audibly—and quietly reflect on them, a phrase here and there will prompt a memory of the way the confession of a particular Lord's Day seemed to express their own sense of need, or how the words of assurance brought a fresh sense of God's pardoning love. But for every reader, this book gives expression to our deepest needs for forgiveness and assurance. It helps us to discover afresh that God's grace is all-sufficient for us because it reminds us that in Jesus Christ the Heavenly Father has given us a loving Savior, and by His Spirit reassures us that there is forgiveness.

I will never forget a text message I received one Saturday evening in 2011, at the end of the two days that the church's search committee had spent talking with (and no doubt seeking to "woo") Derek and Rosemary. That afternoon, as our friends left to return to Jackson ("home" as it was then), I wondered if any of the committee believed they would see the Thomases again! But then came the text. "I can hardly believe it," Derek wrote, "I think we're coming!" The rest, as they say, is history—but what a wonderful and blessed history it has been!

Our Confession of Faith tells us that "the efficacy [the blessing] of baptism is not tied to that moment of time wherein it is administered." It lingers on. And thankfully, that is also true of the entirety of Derek's ministry. It applies to the twelve plus years between 2011 and 2023, during which he has preached and taught, challenged, and directed, comforted, and strengthened, and to the hundreds of Sundays and Wednesdays, and the several thousand other days of his ministry. The fruit of these years "will remain" just as Jesus promised. Indeed it will last into eternity, in our hearts and lives.

Derek has preached about faith and his sermons have been filled with hope. These will indeed "abide." "But the greatest of these is love" (I Cor 13:13). Even when the pastoral relationship belongs to the past, that love will endure. And these pages will serve as a permanent token of the mutual love that has made the bond between Derek and Rosemary Thomas and the First Presbyterian Church Family so richly blessed.

Sinclair B. Ferguson

Introduction

Derek W.H. Thomas was called to be the Minister of Preaching and Teaching at First Presbyterian Church in Columbia, South Carolina on March 27, 2011, and he began his ministry there in June 2011. A short time later, in August 2013, he was called to be the Senior Minister of this church following the retirement of Sinclair B. Ferguson.

A special and consistent part of the Sunday morning worship service at First Presbyterian is the Corporate Prayer of Confession and Assurance of Pardon, which typically comes immediately before the pastoral prayer. In the confession, the congregation collectively acknowledges before our Heavenly Father that, every day, we have fallen short of what He requires of us, in thought, word, and deed, and have fallen short of the glory of God. Then, in the assurance of pardon, the minister reminds us that God, by making His son Jesus Christ the propitiation for our sins, has forgiven us and treats us as holy and blameless before His judgment seat.

During the latter years of his service as the Senior Minister, Dr. Thomas began personally to write the corporate confessions and assurances of pardon. Most frequently, the confessions and assurances of pardon Dr. Thomas wrote each week drew from his sermon, connecting this moment of corporate prayer with the Scripture he was about to unpack for the congregation.

Dr. Thomas's loving service as a preacher and pastor molded and encouraged the congregation of First Presbyterian. As the church reflected on Dr. Thomas's retirement, it recognized that these corporate confessions and assurances of pardon will be dearly missed. And it realized that the confessions and assurances Dr. Thomas prepared are too significant to remain only in the bulletins of Sunday morning services.

The church therefore compiled these confessions and assurances and put them into this book with valuable insight and guidance from Dr. Sinclair B. Ferguson. They are divided into thirteen chapters, each addressing a different need or occasion for confessing our sin. Our prayer is that not only members of our church, but also Christians around the world, will find this book a helpful guide for falling on their knees in prayer, confessing their sins, and having confidence that Jesus' death and resurrection is sufficient for salvation.

From a grateful congregation

Chapter 1
Confessions of Apathy

When we remember that the omnipotent God who created the universe loved us so much that He sent His only Son to suffer the punishment for our sins, we respond with worship and adoration of Him. We must run to Jesus and away from our sin. But far too often, we do not treat sin as the grave issue it really is. Sin deserves the eternal wrath of a just and holy God. We, however, ignore our sin or treat it as a trifling inconvenience to do away with. Or worse, we can even pamper it and help it grow. In these confessions, Dr. Thomas reminds us to hate and grieve over our sins, as we ask God to help us root them out of our lives.

May 29, 2022

Sermon
"I Want Those You Have Given Me...to See My Glory"
John 17:20-26

CORPORATE PRAYER OF CONFESSION

Heavenly Father, your Word tells us clearly that we are to "put to death the deeds of the body." We are to say "No" to sin in its first inklings in our minds. We are to do this every day, and the cost will involve pain and anguish. But too often, we grant the sin time to breathe and grow. Too often, we allow it time to manifest itself in words and deeds that offend you. Too often, we convince ourselves that this is only a small sin, and indulgence for a moment will not harm us or others. Help us be prepared to pluck out our eyes and sever hands and feet as Jesus commanded. And today, help us to identify and destroy our besetting sins. In the name of Jesus. Amen.

(based on Matthew 5:29; Romans 8:13; and Hebrews 12:1)

ASSURANCE OF PARDON

Who is a God like you, pardoning iniquity
   and passing over transgression
   for the remnant of his inheritance?
He does not retain his anger forever,
   because he delights in steadfast love.
He will again have compassion on us;
   he will tread our iniquities underfoot.
You will cast all our sins
   into the depths of the sea.

(Micah 7:18-19)

September 4, 2022

Sermon
"From Darkness to Light"
Colossians 1:13-14

CORPORATE PRAYER OF CONFESSION

Your Word exhorts us to "put to death the deeds of the body." Too often we have pampered our besetting sins, allowing them room to breathe and prosper. We have played games, pretending that these sins are relatively minor and harmless. Remind us, O Lord, that it was for these very sins that Christ shed His blood to atone for us. That Jesus likened mortification to plucking out eyes and severing arms tells us so dramatically that killing sin—our sin—is difficult. It feels as though we are destroying a part of who we are. But this is not who we are! We are Christians, in union and communion with Jesus Christ. Grant us the strength and resolve to be killing sin every day, until you take us home. In Jesus' name. Amen.

(based on Romans 8:13)

ASSURANCE OF PARDON

Therefore, since we have been justified by faith, we have peace with God through our Lord Jesus Christ.

(Romans 5:1)

January 15, 2023

Sermon
"The Meaning of Baptism"
Colossians 2:11-12

CORPORATE PRAYER OF CONFESSION

Heavenly Father, help us see our sins as you see them—as the spiritual equivalent of dirt that needs to be washed and cleansed. Help us confess our secret sins and grant us a passionate desire to see them destroyed. Provide for us daily strength to mortify "the deeds of the body" for your Word tells us that "if you live according to the flesh you will die." In Jesus' name. Amen.

(based on Romans 8:13 and I Peter 3:21)

ASSURANCE OF PARDON

A debtor to mercy alone,
Of covenant mercy I sing,
Nor fear, with God's righteousness on,
My person and off'rings to bring.
The terrors of law and of God
With me can have nothing to do;
My Savior's obedience and blood
Hide all my transgressions from view.

(Augustus Toplady, "A Debtor to Mercy Alone", stanza 1)

June 7, 2020

Sermon
"Paul: The Lord Stood by Me"
II Timothy 4:9-18

CORPORATE PRAYER OF CONFESSION
AND ASSURANCE OF PARDON

Heavenly Father, we are grateful that you do not allow us to be at peace when we stray from you. Our conscience nags at us. We feel that inward ache that says something is wrong. Our bones seem to waste away. Guilty feelings oppress us.

Still, we are experts at pretending that all is fine. So we beg you not to let up. Keep your hand heavy upon us, pressing us down to our knees to confess our sins and plead for mercy. The pain of it is, surprisingly, a gracious thing, for in the sense of guilt we sense that we are your children, and that you care enough to chastise us.

Thank you for your forgiveness. It comes at such a price—the life and death of your Son, our Savior, Jesus Christ. Thank you that you made Him, who knew no sin, to be sin for us that we might be reckoned the righteousness of God in Him.

Hear us as we now confess our sins in these moments of silence.

(based on Psalm 32)

July 5, 2020

Sermon
"Procrastination"
Haggai 1:1-2

CORPORATE PRAYER OF CONFESSION

Almighty and most merciful Father, we rejoice in your mercy; it is higher than the heavens, deeper than the sea, wider than our wanderings, greater than all our sin. Forgive our careless attitude toward your sovereign design for us, our complaining when in trial, our envy of the perceived well-being of others, our obsession with pleasing ourselves, our indifference to the needs of others, our neglect of your commands. Help us to repent of these transgressions and seek you with all our heart, so that we might walk in your ways, until you call us home. Amen.

ASSURANCE OF PARDON

"Yet even now," declares the Lord,
    "return to me with all your heart,
with fasting, with weeping, and with mourning;
    and rend your hearts and not your garments."
Return to the LORD your God,
    for he is gracious and merciful,
slow to anger, and abounding in steadfast love;
    and he relents over disaster.

(Joel 2:12-13)

November 1, 2020

Sermon
"Hitting Rock Bottom"
Luke 22:31-34

CORPORATE PRAYER OF CONFESSION

Heavenly Father, your Word tells us that we need to look carefully at how we walk, not as unwise but as wise, making the best use of the time, because the days are evil. We need the wisdom of Solomon to navigate our lives in this season of tension and difficulty. Help us to live according to the rule that "right now counts forever." This moment we have right now, all of the opportunities to do good, will be gone tomorrow. If we waste it, we cannot get it back. We are walking into a battle. We can smell the smoke. All around us are the explosions of hand-grenades. And we have wasted so many opportunities. We haven't redeemed the time. Too often, we have resigned to gloom and doom. We have failed to apply the victory of Jesus to every situation. We have let the devil walk in and cripple us. Lord, by the power of the Holy Spirit, help us to be smarter. For Jesus' sake. Amen.

(based on Ephesians 5:15-16)

ASSURANCE OF PARDON

Whoever conceals his transgressions will not prosper,
but he who confesses and forsakes them will obtain mercy.

(Proverbs 28:13)

June 28, 2020

Sermon
"The First Formal Worship Service after the Exile (Part I)"
Nehemiah 8:1-8

CORPORATE PRAYER OF CONFESSION
AND ASSURANCE OF PARDON

Rise, my soul, to watch and pray, from thy sleep awaken;
Be not by the evil day unawares o'er taken.
For the foe, well we know, oft his harvest reapeth
While the Christian sleepeth.

Lord, we know it all too well that we often drift away from you and fall in love with this present evil world. We have sometimes felt that the "evil day" is upon us—a day when Satan seems to prowl around like a roaring lion seeking whom he may devour. Forgive us for our failure to persevere, our failure to watch and pray, our propensity to fall into temptation again and again. Shake us so that we wake up to the brevity of time and grant us the fullness of the Spirit so that we may lay aside every weight and sin, which cling so closely, and let us run with endurance the race that is set before us, looking to Jesus, the founder and perfecter of our faith. Wash us in the blood of Christ that cleanses from all sin. Amen.

(based on Johann B. Freistein, "Rise, My Soul to Watch and Pray", trans. Catherine Winkworth)

August 2, 2020

Sermon
"If God Is with Us"
Haggai 2:1-5

CORPORATE PRAYER OF CONFESSION

Almighty God, since you delay with so much forbearance the punishments we so much deserve, and daily draw on ourselves, grant that we may not indulge ourselves, but carefully consider how often and in how many different ways we have provoked your wrath against us. May we learn humbly to present ourselves to you for pardon and with true repentance implore your mercy. With all our heart, we desire to submit ourselves to you, whether you chastise us or, according to your infinite goodness, forgive us. Let our condition be ever blessed, not by flattering ourselves in our apathy, but by finding you to be our kind and generous Father, reconciled to us in your only begotten Son, Jesus Christ our Lord. Amen.

ASSURANCE OF PARDON

Therefore, since we have been justified by faith, we have peace with God through our Lord Jesus Christ.

(Romans 5:1)

November 7, 2021

Sermon
"Persecution"
Psalm 69

CORPORATE PRAYER OF CONFESSION

Heavenly Father, you command us in Scripture to "mortify the deeds of the flesh." But we so often find this a difficult thing to do. Sin does not want to die, and killing it seems like a life-long project. Our feeble attempts are too often accompanied by moaning and groaning on our part. Jesus tells us that it is like cutting off an arm or plucking out an eye. It feels as if we are saying goodbye to something we think we cannot live without. We know that outward acts of sin and rebellion begin with a desire in the mind. Help us to purify our desires. Help, by the help of the Holy Spirit, to kill sin at its very inception. Help us break the habit of sin so that we may become more and more like Jesus. It is in His powerful name that we ask this. Amen.

ASSURANCE OF PARDON

I lay my sins on Jesus, the spotless Lamb of God;
He bears them all, and frees us from the accursed load:
I bring my guilt to Jesus, to wash my crimson stains
White in his blood most precious, till not a spot remains.

(Horatius Bonar, "I Lay My Sins on Jesus", stanza 1)

January 23, 2022

Sermon
"The Beginning of Everything"
Genesis 1:1-25

CORPORATE PRAYER OF CONFESSION

Lord, you created us in your image and after your likeness, but we defaced the beauty of what you made and threw it away. We were created to explore and discover and form beautiful relationships and take care of this world, but we have used what we have discovered to destroy rather than beautify. We were created to be holy, but we preferred to rebel than to obey, to create idols rather than worship you. We thank you that you have quickened us in Christ and that our "new self" is "being renewed in knowledge after the image of its creator." Forgive us for the lack of progress we have shown in this renewal. Persevere with us to the end and do not forsake us. In Jesus' name. Amen.

ASSURANCE OF PARDON

"I will never leave you nor forsake you."

(Hebrews 13:5, citing Joshua 1:5)

Chapter 2
Confessions of Doubt

God is our loving Heavenly Father. As Jesus explained to His disciples after teaching them how to pray, if our earthly fathers would give us a fish instead of a serpent, how much more will our Heavenly Father give to His children when they ask. Yet we frequently doubt God's goodness, love, mercy, and providence. These confessions allow us to acknowledge our doubt, as the assurances remind us that we have been adopted as sons and daughters of God.

February 7, 2021

Sermon
"Far from Home"
Psalm 42

CORPORATE PRAYER OF CONFESSION
AND ASSURANCE OF PARDON

Heavenly Father, your tender care over us overwhelms our hearts every day. But as we come to you today, we confess that sometimes we do not feel your embrace. Sometimes we have felt down, in the blues, in Doubting Castle, surrounded by fog and uncertainty. How we thank you for today's two psalms in which the psalmist confesses to feeling "forsaken" by friends, by family, but, most especially, by you! We know that you never forsake us, but we are weak and feeble, and we sometimes succumb to the dark side. Sometimes we simply do not know the reason—and we thank you for counselors, medicine, and friends who help us persevere in the darkness. Most of all, we thank you that in the dungeon of despair, our Savior is right beside us, and we need only to reach out and grasp hold of His hand. In Jesus' name. Amen.

November 21, 2021

Sermon
"A Psalm for Old Age"
Psalm 71

CORPORATE PRAYER OF CONFESSION

The psalm we study today shows an elderly believer still strong in the faith. Experiencing trials has not made him bitter or grumpy. Daily he takes refuge in you, O Lord. You remain his hope and trust. He remains joyful and full of faith. Forgive us, O Lord, when we seem to be crushed by trials, and the root of bitterness begins to grow. Grant us grace to repent today and be strong in the Lord and in the power of your might. For Jesus' sake. Amen.

ASSURANCE OF PARDON

For the wages of sin is death, but the free gift of God is eternal life in Christ Jesus our Lord.

(Romans 6:23)

June 4, 2023

Sermon
"A Valentine Card from Heaven"
Zephaniah 3:17

CORPORATE PRAYER OF CONFESSION

Heavenly Father, too often we forget that you are near. We pout and feel sorry for ourselves, thinking we must carry the burden alone. When our sins overwhelm us, we conclude we are unlovable, but you love us always, "you rejoice over (us) with gladness." Enable us each to live as one who has been loved from before the foundation of the world. In Jesus' name. Amen.

(based on Zephaniah 3:17 and Ephesians 1:4)

ASSURANCE OF PARDON

Loved with everlasting love,
Led by grace that love to know;
Spirit, breathing from above,
Thou hast taught me it is so.
Oh, this full and perfect peace!
Oh, this transport all divine!
In a love which cannot cease,
I am His, and He is mine.

(George W. Robinson, "Loved with Everlasting Love", stanza 1)

Chapter 3
Confessions of Faithlessness

At its simplest, the gospel is a remarkable story: God so loved His people that He sent His Son into the world to die an agonizing death as the propitiation for our sins and to rise from the dead as our Savior. We therefore have every reason to be grateful, and our lives should reflect a commitment to walking in His light. Yet every day, we fail to do so. This chapter helps us confess our faithlessness and know that our Heavenly Father will welcome us, the prodigal children, home.

December 22, 2019

Sermon
"Thou Who Wast Rich Beyond All Measure"
II Corinthians 8:9

CONFESSION OF SIN

O my Savior, come to me.
I am slow to learn, prone to forget, and weak to climb;
I am in the foothills when I should be on the heights;
I am pained by my graceless heart,
  my prayerless days,
  my poverty of love,
  my sloth in the heavenly race,
  my blemished conscience,
  my wasted hours,
  my missed opportunities.
I am often blind while the light shines around me:
take the scales from my eyes,
grind to dust my heart of unbelief.
Do whatever it takes to set me on fire for you.
Make it my highest joy to know you,
  meditate on you,
  gaze on you,
  sit like Mary at your feet,
  lean like John on your breast,
  appeal like Peter to your love,
  count like Paul all things as rubbish in comparison to
  you.
I believe; help my unbelief. Amen.

ASSURANCE OF PARDON

If God is for us, who can be against us? He who did not spare his own Son but gave him up for us all, how will he not also with him graciously give us all things?

(Romans 8:31b-32)

January 5, 2020

Sermon
"Wanted: Dead or Alive!"
John 18:1-27

CONFESSION OF SIN

Heavenly Father, for the blessedness of the gospel, we thank you; for the assurance of forgiveness, we adore you; for our right to call you ABBA, Father, we delight in you.

There is no one like you; in your majesty, you rule over all things, you order our steps, you guide and provide, guard and protect.

You know our sins, and you do not shame us. You know our weaknesses, and yet you do not despise us. You know our sorrows, and you lift us into your tender embrace. You know our besetting sins, and yet you are patient—"slow to anger, abounding in love and faithfulness."

We ask today again for forgiveness for our many sins: thoughtless words that caused hurt to another, opportunities to do good that we failed to grasp, neglect in prayer, unbelief when we encountered obstacles in our path, irritation with a friend's failures, and so much more. Forgive us, dear Lord, for thinking of ourselves more highly than we ought and thinking of others less compassionately than they deserve.

At the beginning of a New Year, we resolve to run with endurance the race that is set before us, looking unto Jesus, the founder and perfecter of our faith. We resolve to bookend what time we have with gospel-centered motivations.

Have mercy on us. We build our lives on nothing less than Jesus' blood and righteousness. Amen.

ASSURANCE OF PARDON

The LORD is merciful and gracious,
  slow to anger and abounding in steadfast love.
He will not always chide,
  nor will he keep his anger forever.
He does not deal with us according to our sins,
  nor repay us according to our iniquities.
For as high as the heavens are above the earth,
  so great is his steadfast love toward those who fear him;
as far as the east is from the west,
  so far does he remove our transgressions from us.

(Psalm 103:8-12)

February 2, 2020

Sermon
"Conjuring Trick with Bones"
John 20:1-10

CORPORATE PRAYER OF CONFESSION AND ASSURANCE OF PARDON

Heavenly Father, as we come to you today, we affirm that we are sinners by nature and by deed. Our personal sins are great; they are a burden to us. They diminish us and impair our vision of you. Sometimes it feels like we are carrying around a heavy sack of sand upon our backs. We remember in Proverbs where it tells us that sexual sin is the equivalent of being shot in the liver by an arrow! We are such rebels. When we refuse to heed you and lean into our sins, pushing the boundaries a little more each time, we alienate ourselves from you. We have felt your hand and our conscience warns us of your hostility. We grieve the Holy Spirit.

What a relief repentance brings! How simple it is and yet how hard! We turn away from our sins this morning and turn towards you. We behold your beautiful face smiling upon us and your arms outstretched to receive us in your embrace. Our sins, though they be red like crimson, are covered, hidden from your sight forever. Our transgressions are laid on our substitute—our Lord and Savior, Jesus Christ. "[I]n my place condemned he stood; Sealed my pardon with his blood."

Blessed is the one whose transgression is forgiven, whose sin is covered. And in Christ, we are blessed indeed. Hear us, O Lord, in Jesus' name. Amen.

(based on Psalm 32; Proverbs 7:23; and Philip P. Bliss,
"Man of Sorrows! What a Name")

February 16, 2020

Sermon
"Doubting Thomas"
John 20:24-31

CORPORATE PRAYER OF CONFESSION
AND ASSURANCE OF PARDON

Heavenly Father, Scripture tells us that if we confess our sins, you are faithful and just to forgive us our sins and cleanse us from all unrighteousness. That you are faithful to your promises, we understand. But how can it be "just" to forgive us our sins? Surely, the just thing would be to punish us, to give us what we deserve, and cast us from your presence forever! The just thing is for your anger to be kindled and your wrath to be poured out upon us. But when we reason this way, we forget the gospel. Our sins were laid upon your Son. He was made sin for us. You poured on Him what our sins deserved. He atoned for our sins by becoming our substitute. In Christ, our sins have been dealt with, and there is nothing to be afraid of. He satisfied the demands of divine justice. For His sake, you are bound to forgive us. It is the just thing to do.

Heavenly Father, the gospel is such a beautiful thing! Help us today to grasp its beauty for Jesus' sake. Amen.

(based on I John 1:9)

March 8, 2020

Sermon
"Absalom"
II Samuel 13:1-39

CORPORATE PRAYER OF CONFESSION
AND ASSURANCE OF PARDON

The Bible is very clear that all of us have sinned. There is only one person who has never sinned—Jesus Christ our Lord and Savior. He was harmless and undefiled and separate from sinners. But we sin all the time, in thought, word, and deed. We fall short of the glory of God. We fail to be what you intended us to be. We reach out for it, but we stumble and fall all the time. All our efforts to save ourselves miss the mark. We cannot earn your approval. Our lives are stained by sin. But thank you, Heavenly Father, for sending your Son to die for us, to pay the penalty for sin in our stead. Thank you for the assurance that, in Christ, we are reckoned as pure and spotless as He is. We come to you now, clothed in the spotless garments of our Savior, and we know we are welcome. Amen.

(based on Romans 3:23)

April 12, 2020

Sermon
"When You're Down, You Don't Think Straight"
Luke 24:13-24

CORPORATE PRAYER OF CONFESSION
AND ASSURANCE OF PARDON

Gracious Heavenly Father, this morning we especially remember that you sent your only Son to die in our place and to rise again for our justification. And we remember the words of the apostle, "We know that our old self was crucified with him in order that the body of sin might be brought to nothing, so that we would no longer be enslaved to sin." Too often we find ourselves serving sin as though we were its slave when, in truth, we owe no allegiance to it. Too often we have chosen to remain captive to doubt and fear and ways that lead to death. By our thoughts, words, and actions, we have scorned your love, diminished the lives of others, and defaced your image in us. Forgive us, we pray, and help us rest in the assurance that in Christ, we truly are forgiven—totally, and forever. Amen.

(based on Romans 4:25 and 6:6)

April 19, 2020

Sermon
"Joseph: God's Ways Are Not Our Ways"
Genesis 39

CORPORATE PRAYER OF CONFESSION
AND ASSURANCE OF PARDON

Heavenly Father, all of us are guilty of Adam's first transgression. As our representative, when he fell, we fell with him. When he failed to present a perfect righteousness, he became utterly indisposed, disabled, and made opposite to all that is spiritually good, and wholly inclined to all evil, and that continually. From this condition proceed all actual transgressions. This was our condition by birth, but grace found us. We discovered a Savior whose obedience was reckoned to our account. He rescued and redeemed us, and we are thankful beyond words. We have been baptized into Christ, into His death and resurrection. We bless you this morning that, in Christ, we are children of God, heirs of God and joint heirs with Jesus Christ. Amen.

(based on Westminster Larger Catechism Answer 25)

June 21, 2020

CORPORATE PRAYER OF CONFESSION
AND ASSURANCE OF PARDON

Lord Jesus, when you showed yourself to the prophet, Isaiah, as one who is utterly holy, his response was to say, "Woe is me! I am undone, because I am a man of unclean lips, and I dwell in the midst of a people of unclean lips: for mine eyes have seen the King, the LORD of hosts." He had the cleanest lips in Israel, but in your holy presence, he felt unclean and sinful. How much more so for us! As we come before you now, we tremble because our sins rise up and condemn us, but your Word assures us that you are "faithful and just to forgive us our sins and to cleanse us from all unrighteousness." How blessed we are. How gracious you are. We worship you. Amen.

(based on Isaiah 6:5 and I John 1:9)

July 12, 2020

Sermon
"God's House or Mine"
Haggai 1:3-11

CORPORATE PRAYER OF CONFESSION

Heavenly Father, we are gathered before you, maker of heaven and earth, in the assurance that you promised to dwell with the broken and contrite of spirit, to confess that we have sinned in thought, word, and deed; we have not loved you with all our heart and mind and soul and strength; we have not loved our neighbor as ourselves. We have not prayed as we ought nor read and pondered your Word as we ought; we have said things we should not have said and been silent when we should have spoken. In your mercy, deepen our sorrow, grant us the grace to repent in a manner that is godly. Restore to us the joy of our salvation so that we may love you more and more. Amen.

ASSURANCE OF PARDON

For God so loved the world, that he gave his only Son, that whoever believes in him should not perish but have eternal life.

(John 3:16)

October 18, 2020

Sermon
"Let Us Make Tents"
Luke 9:28-36, II Peter 2:13-21

CORPORATE PRAYER OF CONFESSION

Heavenly Father, we come before you with the words of the psalmist on our lips:

> Where shall I go from your Spirit?
> Or where shall I flee from your presence?
>   If I ascend to heaven, you are there!
> If I make my bed in Sheol, you are there!
>   If I take the wings of the morning
> and dwell in the uttermost parts of the sea,
>   even there your hand shall lead me,
> and your right hand shall hold me.
>   If I say, "Surely the darkness shall cover me,
> and the light about me be night,"
>   even the darkness is not dark to you;
> the night is bright as the day,
> for darkness is as light with you.

There is absolutely nothing that is hidden from you. We may fool others, but we cannot fool you. You know us completely and we cannot hide our sins from you. You have observed our shortcomings this week: deceptions, lies, gossip, hurtful words, inappropriate responses, failures to act, and so much more. Have mercy on us, O Lord. In Jesus' Name. Amen.

(based on Psalm 139)

ASSURANCE OF PARDON

If we confess our sins, he is faithful and just to forgive us our sins and to cleanse us from all unrighteousness.

(I John 1:9)

March 14, 2021

Sermon
"The City of God"
Psalm 48

CORPORATE PRAYER OF CONFESSION

Heavenly Father, grant me a deeper sense of my unworthiness that I may delight in your forgiveness. Show me my sin that I may gaze more lovingly at my Savior. Open up the darkest wells of my heart so that I may feel again that Christ's blood covers it all. Deepen my repentance that I may run all the harder toward you. Plough up the soil of my flesh that by your grace seeds of holiness will grow to honor you. For Jesus' sake. Amen.

ASSURANCE OF PARDON

If we confess our sins, he is faithful and just to forgive us our sins and to cleanse us from all unrighteousness.

(I John 1:9)

March 21, 2021

Sermon
"The World's Empty Glory"
Psalm 49

CORPORATE PRAYER OF CONFESSION

O Father, we are gathered before you, the maker of heaven and earth, whose chosen dwelling place is with the broken and contrite. We confess that we have sinned in thought and word and deed; we have not loved you with all our heart and soul; we have not loved you with all our mind and strength; we have not even loved our neighbor as ourselves.

In your mercy, deepen our sorrow for the sin that remains in our hearts. Teach us to hate our sin with a holy hatred. Amen.

ASSURANCE OF PARDON

I acknowledged my sin to you,
and I did not cover my iniquity;
I said, "I will confess my transgressions to the Lord,"
and you forgave the iniquity of my sin.

(Psalm 32:5)

April 25, 2021

Sermon
"Serpent's Brood"
Psalm 53

CORPORATE PRAYER OF CONFESSION

Today's psalm tells us "there is none that does good, not even one." And Paul, citing this verse in Romans, concludes that "by works of the law no human being will be justified in his sight, since through the law comes knowledge of sin." Heavenly Father, had you not saved us, we would still be dead in trespasses and sins. We would be without hope in this world and the one to come. Sadly, even though we are your redeemed children, we still sin; we continue to listen to the lies of Satan and obey sin's bidding. Forgive us, we pray. In Jesus' name. Amen.

(based on Psalms 14 and 53 and
Romans 3:12, 20)

ASSURANCE OF PARDON

Therefore, since we have been justified by faith, we have peace with God through our Lord Jesus Christ.

(Romans 5:1)

May 2, 2021

Sermon
"My Helper"
Psalm 54

CORPORATE PRAYER OF CONFESSION

Heavenly Father, once again we come to confess our sins before you. Sin is deceitful: it promises reward but, in reality, it brings deceit, promises joy but instead brings misery and shame, allures with promises of benefit but ruins and destroys us. The good we would, we do not, and the evil that we would not, we do. O wretched people that we are! Cleanse us afresh in the atoning blood of our precious Savior, Jesus Christ. Amen.

ASSURANCE OF PARDON

Thy work alone, O Christ, can ease this weight of sin;
Thy blood alone, O Lamb of God, can give me peace within.
Thy love to me, O God, not mine, O Lord, to thee,
Can rid me of this dark unrest, and set my spirit free.

(Horatius Bonar, "Not What My Hands Have Done", stanza 2)

Sermon
"Betrayed"
Psalm 55

CORPORATE PRAYER OF CONFESSION

O Lord, the great and awesome God, who keeps covenant and steadfast love with those who love him and keep his commandments, we have sinned and done wrong and acted wickedly and rebelled, turning aside from your commandments and rules. We have not listened to your servants the prophets, who spoke in your name to our kings, our princes, and our fathers, and to all the people of the land. To you, O Lord, belongs righteousness, but to us, open shame, as at this day, to the men of Judah, to the inhabitants of Jerusalem, and to all Israel, those who are near and those who are far away, in all the lands to which you have driven them, because of the treachery that they have committed against you. To us, O Lord, belongs open shame, to our kings, to our princes, and to our fathers, because we have sinned against you. To the Lord our God belong mercy and forgiveness, for we have rebelled against him and have not obeyed the voice of the Lord our God by walking in his laws, which he set before us by his servants the prophets.

(Daniel 9:4b-10)

ASSURANCE OF PARDON

Whoever conceals his transgressions will not prosper, but he who confesses and forsakes them will obtain mercy.

(Proverbs 28:13)

May 23, 2021

Sermon
"Saved to Sing"
Psalm 57

CORPORATE PRAYER OF CONFESSION

Heavenly Father, our sins are too heavy for us to carry. They are a burden that weighs us down. We need to rid ourselves of this incumbrance. Like Bunyan's Pilgrim, we want to see this load rolling down the hill and disappearing into the sepulcher. Forgive what we tremble to confess. Liberate us from the past which we cannot change. Help us by your Holy Spirit to discover afresh the freedom that is to be found in Christ alone. Amen.

ASSURANCE OF PARDON

Who is a God like you, pardoning iniquity
and passing over transgression
for the remnant of his inheritance?
He does not retain his anger forever,
because he delights in steadfast love.

(Micah 7:18)

August 22, 2021

Sermon
"Vain Is the Help of Man!"
Psalm 60

CORPORATE PRAYER OF CONFESSION
AND ASSURANCE OF PARDON

Bless you, O Lord. All that is within me desires to bless your holy name. My iniquity is great, but you forgive all my iniquity and redeem my life from the pit. Your steadfast love and mercy form a crown around my head. Your love toward me is higher than the tallest mountain, wider than the farthest horizons we can measure. You are like a tender, loving Father toward me. My sins, and they are many, are wiped away; they are gone without trace, irrecoverable, never to be located. Though I may search for them, I cannot find them. They are covered by the blood of Jesus, and there is no love like the love of Jesus. Amen.

(based on Psalm 103)

August 29, 2021

Sermon
"The Rock That Is Higher Than I"
Psalm 61

CORPORATE PRAYER OF CONFESSION
AND ASSURANCE OF PARDON

When confronted by your absolute holiness, the prophet Isaiah cried: "Woe is me! For I am lost (literally, undone); for I am a man of unclean lips." He was keenly aware that at the point of his greatest usefulness—he used his lips as a prophet to proclaim the unsearchable riches of the gospel—he was also a terrible sinner, one who fell short of the glory of God. We sin in our best deeds. Your holiness makes us tremble because in an instant you could banish us from your presence. It is with joy, therefore, that we lay hold of Christ again. He is our salvation. He is our redemption. He is our propitiation. He is our substitute and sin-bearer. As John said, "If we confess our sins, he is faithful and just to forgive us our sins and to cleanse us from all unrighteousness." Amen.

(based on Isaiah 6:5 and I John 1:9)

September 19, 2021

Sermon
"Measure for Measure"
Psalm 64

CORPORATE PRAYER OF CONFESSION

The psalmist tells us that it was "good" for him to be afflicted "that I might learn your statutes." Your statutes are a reflection of what you are. Only a conviction of your steadfast love would induce David to conclude that affliction was good for him. Too often we attempt almost anything to avoid affliction rather than accepting it as a way of getting to know you better. All of our afflictions are as your beloved children. They come, not to harm us as much as to humble us, and make us yearn for you more and more. Forgive us, O Lord, when we have bristled at your providence. In Jesus' name. Amen.

(based on Psalm 119:71)

ASSURANCE OF PARDON

Blessed is the one whose transgression is forgiven,
whose sin is covered.

(Psalm 32:1)

December 26, 2021

Sermon
"The Dark Side of Christmas"
Luke 2:33-35

CORPORATE PRAYER OF CONFESSION

Heavenly Father, our lives are filled with sin.
We forget our neighbor's needs
and do not love you above all else.
We need a Savior.
O come, O come, Emmanuel, and dwell in our hearts. Amen.

ASSURANCE OF PARDON

Comfort, comfort my people, says your God.
Speak tenderly to Jerusalem,
   and cry to her
that her warfare is ended,
   that her iniquity is pardoned,
that she has received from the LORD's hand
   double for all her sins.

(Isaiah 40:1-2)

January 16, 2022

Sermon
"The Church's Members"
Ephesians 4:1-16

CORPORATE PRAYER OF CONFESSION

Merciful Father, you are a just judge. You teach us that every sin, even the least, deserves your wrath and curse. We confess our iniquity. We are sorry for our sin. We do not deserve your love. You command us to worship you alone. Instead, we constantly chase after idols. We love money, possessions, and praise from our peers more than we love you. We are sorry. You graciously invite us to pray. Yet, we neglect prayer because we don't think we need you. We are sorry. You command us to love our neighbor. Instead, we have hated our neighbor. Instead of looking out for the interest of others, we look out for our own interests. We are sorry.

We have nothing to bring before your throne. We are guilty, and we cannot do anything to earn forgiveness. Jesus is our only hope of forgiveness. We believe, Lord. Help our unbelief. Help us look to Jesus. Cleanse our hearts so that we desire to live for you. Give us grace to live as your children. Help us glorify you in everything we think, in everything we say, and in everything we do. We pray this in Jesus' name. Amen.

ASSURANCE OF PARDON

But when the goodness and loving kindness of God our Savior appeared, he saved us, not because of works done by us in righteousness, but according to his own mercy, by the washing of regeneration and renewal of the Holy Spirit, whom he poured out on us richly through Jesus Christ our Savior, so that being justified by his grace we might become heirs according to the hope of eternal life. (Titus 3:4-7)

January 30, 2022

Sermon
"The Crown Jewel of Creation"
Genesis 1:26-31

CORPORATE PRAYER OF CONFESSION

Lord, we were born sinners, and even now, justified in Christ, we remain sinners still. Forgive us, we pray. Amen.

ASSURANCE OF PARDON

My little children, I am writing these things to you so that you may not sin. But if anyone does sin, we have an advocate with the Father, Jesus Christ the righteous.

(I John 2:1)

February 6, 2022

Sermon
"Another Creation Account? Not Really"
Genesis 2:4-25

CORPORATE PRAYER OF CONFESSION

Sin is any want of conformity unto or transgression of the Law of God. There are a multitude of ways in which we have fallen short of your Law. Principally we have failed to love you with all our heart, mind, and soul, and we have equally failed to love our neighbor as ourselves. And your Word reminds us that "the works of the flesh" consist of unclean thoughts, a spirit of enmity, endlessly causing strife, jealousy, fits of anger, envy, and much more. Come, Holy Spirit, and complete what you have begun and make us more like Jesus every day. In Jesus' name. Amen.

(based on Galatians 5:19 and Westminster Shorter Catechism Answer 14)

ASSURANCE OF PARDON

The LORD is merciful and gracious,
    slow to anger and abounding in steadfast love.
He will not always chide,
    nor will he keep his anger forever.
He does not deal with us according to our sins,
    nor repay us according to our iniquities.
For as high as the heavens are above the earth,
    so great is his steadfast love toward those who fear him;
as far as the east is from the west,
    so far does he remove our transgressions from us.

(Psalm 103:8-12)

April 10, 2022

Sermon
"The Entry of the King"
Matthew 21:1-11, 23:37-39

CORPORATE PRAYER OF CONFESSION

Heavenly Father, as the psalmist writes, "Prove me, O LORD, and try me; test my heart and my mind." We confess to you that our faith is weak. We believe; help our unbelief! We have not sufficiently trusted you with our trials and concerns. We have not rested sufficiently in the promises you have made. Nor have we repented of our sins as we should have done. Instead of killing sin, we have fed it and nurtured it and allowed it to grow. You have loved us well, but we have not loved you in return. Too often, our focus has been entirely upon ourselves rather than your glory. Nor have we been humble. We have not emptied ourselves as our Savior did, giving Himself to death for us. Pride raises its ugly head too often. As you examine us today, have mercy upon us and hear our cries for ongoing forgiveness. In the mighty name of Jesus, we pray. Amen.

(based on Psalm 26:2)

ASSURANCE OF PARDON

But God shows his love for us in that while we were still sinners, Christ died for us. Since, therefore, we have now been justified by his blood, much more shall we be saved by him from the wrath of God.

(Romans 5:8-9)

August 7, 2022

Sermon
"A Threefold Blessing"
Colossians 1:1-2

CORPORATE PRAYER OF CONFESSION

Heavenly Father, you have an absolute right to tell how, as Christians, we should live. You require of us holiness. Your Word says, "You shall be holy, as I am holy." This holiness should mark our character and conduct. We should live our whole lives worshiping you and giving thanks to you, separating ourselves from the ways of this world. But we sin every day. We miss the mark and fail to practice righteousness in all our heart and soul. Forgive us, O Lord, and grant us the power of the Holy Spirit to repent. For Jesus' sake. Amen.

(based on I Peter 1:15 and Leviticus 11:14)

ASSURANCE OF PARDON

In him we have redemption through his blood, the forgiveness of our trespasses, according to the riches of his grace.

(Ephesians 1:7)

August 21, 2022

Sermon
"Apostolic Prayer (1)*"*
Colossians 1:9-10

CORPORATE PRAYER OF CONFESSION

Heavenly Father, we do not fear you as we ought. You tell us that we should "work out" our "salvation with fear and trembling." We should reverence you. You do not call upon us to be afraid of you. We are your children, and you desire the best for each one of us. But you are sovereign. Your ways are not our ways, and your thoughts are not our thoughts. You are infinite, eternal, and unchangeable. What we know about you is only what you have revealed. We know a little. We grasp even less. And it is awesome that you work in our hearts as we seek to discern your will and purpose. This knowledge evokes deep awe and praise and a sense of humble dependence upon you. Forgive us when our thoughts about you have been too small. In Jesus' name. Amen.

(based on Philippians 2:12-13)

ASSURANCE OF PARDON

"Behold, God is my salvation;
    I will trust, and will not be afraid;
for the LORD GOD is my strength and my song,
    and he has become my salvation."

With joy you will draw water from the wells of salvation.

(Isaiah 12:2-3)

October 2, 2022

Sermon
"Christ: The Fullness of God"
Colossians 1:19-20

CORPORATE PRAYER OF CONFESSION

Jesus, you taught us to model ourselves after you whenever you said, "Take my yoke upon you, and learn from me." You are the perfect being, and we are imperfect. Yoked to you, linked side by side with you, help us to learn to follow what you do. We have been rebellious far too often. We have strayed from your path and followed the devices and desires of own hearts. Forgive us, O LORD. Help us to keep in step with you. Help us to live beside you, and in you. Then we shall walk in the paths of righteousness. And we shall feel the comfort of your presence. Amen.

(based on Matthew 11:29)

ASSURANCE OF PARDON

Sing aloud, O daughter of Zion;
  shout, O Israel!
Rejoice and exult with all your heart,
  O daughter of Jerusalem!
The Lord has taken away the judgments against you;
  he has cleared away your enemies.
The King of Israel, the Lord, is in your midst;
  you shall never again fear evil.
The LORD your God is in your midst,
  a mighty one who will save;
he will rejoice over you with gladness;
  he will quiet you by his love;
he will exult over you with loud singing.

(Zephaniah 3:14-15, 17)

February 12, 2023

Sermon
"Raised With Christ"
Colossians 3:1-4

CORPORATE PRAYER OF CONFESSION

Heavenly Father, your holiness means that you judge all sin as it deserves, and our conscience affirms that this is proper. Our sins deserve to be punished; they ought to cast us away from your loving presence. There is nothing we can do to erase them. But the penalty that our transgressions deserve was paid in full by our penal substitute and sin-bearer, Jesus Christ. On the cross, He paid the ransom price to set us free. By faith in Him, we are reckoned to be "the righteousness of God." We can scarcely take it in. We thank you in Jesus' name. Amen.

(based on Romans 1:17 and 3:21 and
II Corinthians 5:21)

ASSURANCE OF PARDON

Seek the LORD while he may be found;
    call upon him while he is near;
let the wicked forsake his way,
    and the unrighteous man his thoughts;
let him return to the LORD, that he may have compassion on him,
    and to our God, for he will abundantly pardon.

(Isaiah 55:6-7)

February 26, 2023

Sermon
"Putting Off"
Colossians 3:6-11

CORPORATE PRAYER OF CONFESSION

Heavenly Father, forgive us for being too earthly minded, setting our minds on things that are on earth rather than things that are above. Forgive us when we fail to remember our identity in Christ, living as though we were still in Adam rather than in Christ. Forgive us when we forget that Christ is our life. Help us to put off the old self with its practices and to put on the new self. In Jesus' name. Amen.

ASSURANCE OF PARDON

And we are writing these things so that our joy may be complete. This is the message we have heard from him and proclaim to you, that God is light, and in him is no darkness at all. If we say we have fellowship with him while we walk in darkness, we lie and do not practice the truth. But if we walk in the light, as he is in the light, we have fellowship with one another, and the blood of Jesus his Son cleanses us from all sin.

(I John 1:4-7)

Sermon
"Be Careful When You Say"
Colossians 4:5-6

CORPORATE PRAYER OF CONFESSION

Heavenly Father, we have not always made wise choices. The goals we have set for ourselves have often been worth aiming at. We have not always aimed for your glory. As we have tried to discern your will for us, we have not always chosen the best path. Help us to heed Solomon when he says: "I saw that there is more gain in wisdom than in folly, as there is more gain in light than in darkness. The wise person has his eyes in his head, but the fool walks in darkness." In Jesus' name. Amen.

(Ecclesiastes 2:13-14)

ASSURANCE OF PARDON

God shows his love for us in that while we were still sinners, Christ died for us. Since, therefore, we have now been justified by his blood, much more shall we be saved by him from the wrath of God. For if while we were enemies we were reconciled to God by the death of his Son, much more, now that we are reconciled, shall we be saved by his life.

(Romans 5:8-10)

Chapter 4
Confessions of Fear

Scripture repeatedly teaches us that God has a plan for our lives and holds the universe in the palm of His hand. Even if we can recite these verses, our lives frequently do not bear witness to these truths. We fear for our well-being and the world, being anxious instead of resting in God's providence. Dr. Thomas's confessions in this chapter help give us words to express these shortcomings and offer us renewed assurance that God is sovereign.

March 22, 2020

Sermon
"When the Sky Falls, What Then?"
Job 1

CORPORATE PRAYER OF CONFESSION
AND ASSURANCE OF PARDON

Almighty God, Father of our Lord Jesus Christ, maker of all things, judge of all people, we acknowledge and confess our manifold sins, which we have committed in thought, word, and deed. We confess that we have yielded to fear and a measure of panic as we think about what is happening in the world right now. We have taken our eyes off of you and your power. We have allowed a worldly spirit to engulf us. We have lost the joy of what it means to be a Christian. Forgive us, dear Lord. Fill us with your Spirit. In Jesus' name. Amen.

April 26, 2020

Sermon
"Samson: A Failure's Last Prayer"
Judges 16:23-31

CORPORATE PRAYER OF CONFESSION
AND ASSURANCE OF PARDON

Jesus said, "Do not be anxious about your life," but we have to confess that we have been anxious in recent days. When we watch the news and listen to so-called experts, we are afraid. An invisible virus has us all doing things that go against our natures. And we are dealing with fear and anger. Some of it is understandable, but much of it isn't. Our nerves are on edge. We are frustrated, and we want to be back to where we were a few months ago. And now we fear that we may never get back there, at least not quickly. We want to scream, "This is all so unfair!" We want to cast blame wherever we can, often in a manner that is uncharitable and unchristian. This virus has brought out the best in us, but it has also brought out the worst in us. Forgive us, dear Lord. We are jars of clay and easily broken. But we take refuge that you can make us strong in weakness. Grant us the gift of perseverance right now. And wash us afresh in the blood of Christ whose atoning and substitutionary death assures us that we are your children, forgiven and justified. Amen.

(based on Matthew 6:25)

May 24, 2020

"John the Baptist: Losing's One's Faith and Losing One's Head"
Luke 7:18-23, Mark 6:14-29

CORPORATE PRAYER OF CONFESSION
AND ASSURANCE OF PARDON

Lord Jesus, you told your disciples in the Upper Room, "Let not your hearts be troubled. Believe in God; believe also in me." When you laid down your life for us and afterwards men buried you in a tomb, the disciples were locked up and frightened. They were afraid for their lives. Some of us have had moments when we have felt as though we were locked inside our homes and frightened. But Christians shouldn't live with fear. We should be cautious, but not afraid. We need to trust you more. Forgive us when we see the trial greater than we see you. Help us to look to you, as though looking at the sun, and then everything else will disappear in the sight of your glory. Fill us with the assurance that we are your forgiven children. Amen.

(based on John 14:1)

August 23, 2020

Sermon
"Curses Turned into Blessings"
Haggai 2:10-19

CORPORATE PRAYER OF CONFESSION

Heavenly Father, we have sinned in thought, word, and deed. You call upon us to rejoice in the Lord always, but too often we have allowed ourselves to indulge in gloom and doom; you exhort us not to be anxious about anything, but to commit our concerns to you in prayer with thanksgiving. But too often, prayer has turned into a litany of complaints and fear. You exhort us to stand firm, but too often we have turned and run in cowardice; you call us to a life of contentment, but we have often been the very opposite, wallowing in unhappiness and grievance. We are fickle, and we know it. We confess our sins and ask for a spirit of repentance in Jesus' name. Amen.

(based on Philippians 4)

ASSURANCE OF PARDON

My sin, oh, the bliss of this glorious thought!
My sin, not in part but the whole,
Is nailed to the cross, and I bear it no more,
Praise the Lord, praise the Lord, O my soul!

(Horatio Spafford, "It Is Well with My Soul", stanza 3)

February 21, 2021

Sermon
"Royal Wedding"
Psalm 45

CORPORATE PRAYER OF CONFESSION

Heavenly Father, we confess to knowing Philippians 4:6-7 well when it commands us to be anxious for nothing. But time and again, we fail to heed the command. We fret over things we cannot control. We second-guess decisions we make. And too often, our worry betrays a lack of faith and trust in your goodness and protection. Grant us a fresh glimpse of the crucified Savior, of a love that will not let us go. Help us to view the throne that assures us that you are in complete control of our lives. Restore to us that peace that passes understanding. Guard and protect our lives from the cynicism and lies of Satan. For Jesus' sake. Amen.

ASSURANCE OF PARDON

"Come now, let us reason together, says the LORD:
though your sins are like scarlet,
   they shall be as white as snow;
though they are red like crimson,
   they shall become like wool."

(Isaiah 1:18)

Chapter 5
Confessions of Hypocrisy

A frequent accusation against Christians is that they do not practice what they preach. Sadly, we are often guilty of this charge. In some cases, our hypocrisy is open for all to see. In other cases, our hypocrisy is known only to us. In either situation, our lives do not reflect the gospel. Here, the confessions express our failure to live as we ought, and the assurances remind us of God's forgiveness.

December 15, 2019

Sermon
"While Shepherds Watched Their Flocks"
Luke 2:8-14

CONFESSION OF SIN

Our Father, we confess that we often cleanse the outside of our lives, yet do nothing about the inside of our hearts. Outside we look moral and upright, yet inside we are filled with greed and selfishness. We think we follow your law, yet we neglect justice and your love. We think we deserve positions of honor; we love it when others pay special attention to us. We load people down with impossible demands, and we will not lift one finger to help them. Have mercy on us for being like the Pharisees. May you cleanse us—all of us and all of who we are—from the inside out.

(based on Luke 11:39-46)

ASSURANCE OF PARDON

But God, being rich in mercy, because of the great love with which he loved us, even when we were dead in our trespasses, made us alive together with Christ—by grace you have been saved—and raised us up with him and seated us with him in the heavenly places in Christ Jesus, so that in the coming ages he might show the immeasurable riches of his grace in kindness toward us in Christ Jesus.

(Ephesians 2:4-7)

February 9, 2020

Sermon
"No Need to Cry"
John 20:11-23

CORPORATE PRAYER OF CONFESSION
AND ASSURANCE OF PARDON

Heavenly Father, Paul reminds us that the good we would do, we do not and the evil we would not do, we do. We find ourselves so conflicted: wanting and desiring one thing and practicing another. We want to be kind and gentle, but we often get short and snappy. We say things we regret, do things that later we wish we had not. The flesh lusts against the spirit and the spirit against the flesh—for they seem to be at war with one another. This week has witnessed a catalog of sins, and we are ashamed to declare it yet again to you. We long for a week where we do not have to pray a prayer of confession! But only in heaven will that be so. We do so long for it—and we are blessed above all by the assurance in Jesus Christ, our sins are wiped away—covered by His atoning sacrifice on our behalf. Thank you, Lord Jesus! Amen.

(based on Romans 7:15)

April 5, 2020

Sermon
"Don't Question God's Plan and Purpose. Trust Him Instead"
Job 42:1-6

CORPORATE PRAYER OF CONFESSION
AND ASSURANCE OF PARDON

Heavenly Father, every day I continue to sin in thought, word, and deed. The good I would do, I do not, and the evil I would not, that I find I do. I am such a fool, and none of my sins are hidden from you. We pretend that we can sin in secret when in reality you are watching us the entire time. Forgive us, O Lord. Grant us today renewed gospel conviction to turn from our sins and love you and follow you. In Jesus' name. Amen.

(based on Romans 7:19 and Psalm 69:5)

May 3, 2020

Sermon
"Jeremiah: The Descent into Darkness"
Jeremiah 20

CORPORATE PRAYER OF CONFESSION
AND ASSURANCE OF PARDON

The gospel is for sinners, and that is just what we are. We are justified sinners, reckoned righteous by faith in Jesus, but sinners still. The good we do—and there are things we do that are good—is all tainted by the constant downward drag for self-justification. As the Reformer said, our minds are a perpetual forge of idols. We come to you in prayer, often to be silenced by our unbelief; we read your Word but fail to apply it. We are adept at doing things our way, tuning out the Spirit's leading. Forgive us, dear Lord. Renew us. In the words of the psalmist, restore our souls and grant us the gospel joy of forgiveness, healing, and assurance. In Jesus' name. Amen.

June 14, 2020

Sermon
"John: In the Spirit on the Lord's Day"
Revelation 1

CORPORATE PRAYER OF CONFESSION

Our Father in heaven, we are never more in need of the gospel than right now. Even though we may have been Christians for decades, the remaining sin continues to raise its ugly head and display its power to hoodwink us into believing we must obey its demands. The good we would do, we do not, and the evil we would shun, we do. Sometimes it feels that for every step forward we make in godliness, we take two steps backward. We confess our sins to you—sins of pride, arrogance, discourtesy, dishonesty, selfishness, disloyalty, disrespect, and so much more. May our grief produce a repentance that leads to salvation without regret.

(based on II Corinthians 7:10)

ASSURANCE OF PARDON

There is therefore now no condemnation for those who are in Christ Jesus.

(Romans 8:1)

July 26, 2020

Sermon
"Just Do It"
Haggai 1:12-15

CORPORATE PRAYER OF CONFESSION

Our great and glorious God, loving and gracious Father, we often pretend that we can conceal things from you, conveniently forgetting that you see and know all things. We confess our pride and shortcomings. Gracious God, our sins are too heavy to carry, too real to conceal, too deep to undo. Set us free from a past we cannot change, open to us a future in which we can be changed, and grant us grace to be transformed more and more into the likeness of Jesus. Amen.

ASSURANCE OF PARDON

The soul that on Jesus has leaned for repose,
I will not, I will not desert to his foes;
That soul, though all hell should endeavor to shake,
I'll never, no, never, no, never forsake!

(John Rippon, "How Firm a Foundation", stanza 6)

March 28, 2021

Sermon
"The Judge Breaks Silence"
Psalm 50

CORPORATE PRAYER OF CONFESSION

Heavenly Father, today's psalm tells us that some of our greatest sins take place in this building every Sunday morning: whenever we worship you, but our hearts are not in it; whenever we sing your praises, but we have no idea what we are saying; whenever we listen to your Word, but our minds are in a different place. Help us to repent of our spiritual sins. In Jesus' name. Amen.

ASSURANCE OF PARDON

Our God is full of mercy, slow to anger, and abounding in steadfast love. Through Jesus Christ, we are forgiven. Dare to believe in the gift of a new beginning, and be at peace.

(based on Psalm 86:15)

February 19, 2023

Sermon
"Mortification"
Colossians 3:5

CORPORATE PRAYER OF CONFESSION

Heavenly Father, we confess that we have cravings and habits that have been in us for a long time and need killing. And we confess that this is difficult. Secretly, we don't want them destroyed. We have secretly nurtured and coddled some of these sinful desires. Shockingly, we say one thing and do another. All our outward sins begin their journey in our minds. Our thoughts require cleansing. We practice habits of self-indulgence, and we have become experts in denial, making our sins seem less sinful than they are. Forgive us, O Lord. In Jesus' name. Amen.

(based on Colossians 3:5 and Romans 8:13)

ASSURANCE OF PARDON

Therefore, since we have been justified by faith, we have peace with God through our Lord Jesus Christ.

(Romans 5:1)

Chapter 6
Confessions of Idolatry

As John Calvin famously observed, our hearts are perpetual factories of idols. We, like ancient Israel, chase after false gods and fail to be faithful to the one true God. Dr. Thomas's confessions in this chapter remind us that we repeatedly yearn after everything except what we should. And yet, his assurances remind us, God is always bringing forth the best robe for us when we repent by turning from our sin and toward Him.

March 29, 2020

Sermon
"I Know My Redeemer Lives"
Job 19:20-25

CORPORATE PRAYER OF CONFESSION
AND ASSURANCE OF PARDON

Heavenly Father, you have humbled us in these days. We have worshiped so many idols in our hearts, and you have taken them away. We have worshiped sports, and you have taken it away. We have worshiped our investments and retirement plans, and you have taken them away. We have worshiped Hollywood, and you have taken it away. Have mercy on us for our hearts are a factory of idols. Help us to worship you alone: Father, Son, and Holy Spirit. Help us tear these idols from our breast and worship only you. In Jesus' name. Amen.

Sermon
"When You Hit Rock Bottom"
Jeremiah 20

CORPORATE PRAYER OF CONFESSION

Heavenly Father, when you gave Moses the Ten Commandments, the very first one warned us about idolatry: "You shall have no other gods but me." But no sooner was the Law given than Aaron threw some gold into the furnace and out popped (in his words) a golden calf! And we have been mimicking that ever since. One Reformer wrote that "man's mind is a perpetual factory of idols." Father, we would remind ourselves that an idol is anything to which we give more attention than you. Teach us how to destroy them. Grant us courage to oppose them. Give us resolve to seek you and your kingdom first every day, in every way, for Jesus' sake. Amen.

ASSURANCE OF PARDON

Redeemed, how I love to proclaim it!
Redeemed by the blood of the Lamb;
Redeemed through His infinite mercy,
His child, and forever, I am.

(Fanny Crosby, "Redeemed, How I Love to Proclaim It", stanza 1)

August 28, 2022

Sermon
"Apostolic Prayer (2)"
Colossians 1:11-12

CORPORATE PRAYER OF CONFESSION

The New Testament tells us that the fruit of the Spirit consists in self-control. Without it, we are adrift and subject to all kinds of vice. Without self-control, we are at the mercy of our passions. Idols will manifest themselves and push You aside. Forgive us, Lord, for days when we yield to self-indulgence. Help us to walk with You day by day. Help us to remind ourselves as to who we are in Christ. Aid us to present our bodies a living sacrifice, holy and acceptable to You as an act of worship. In Jesus' name. Amen.

(based on Romans 12:1 and Galatians 5:23)

ASSURANCE OF PARDON

For our sake he made him to be sin who knew no sin, so that in him we might become the righteousness of God.

(II Corinthians 5:21)

October 16, 2022

Sermon
"Reconciliation"
Colossians 1:21-23

CORPORATE PRAYER OF CONFESSION

The psalmist writes, "You make known to me the path of life; in your presence there is fullness of joy; at your right hand are pleasures forevermore." There have been occasions when we have sought our joy in the legitimate things you have given to us without returning thanks to you. Forgive us, O Lord. There have also been occasions when our joy has been sought in illegitimate places. Forgive us, O Lord. Sometimes, something else has gained our full allegiance and pushed you aside. Again, forgive us, O Lord. Help us to bask in the knowledge of your redeeming love for us. Help us to find the fullness of joy in knowing that you will never leave us nor forsake us. In Jesus' name. Amen.

(based on Psalm 16:11)

ASSURANCE OF PARDON

For the wages of sin is death, but the free gift of God is eternal life in Christ Jesus our Lord.

(Romans 6:23)

Chapter 7
Confessions of Impatience

God's ways are higher than our ways, and His thoughts are higher than our thoughts. But we rarely live in light of that reality. We think we know best. We think our plan is right. We therefore fail to be patient and trust in God's loving providence. We do not have faith that our trials are designed to consume our dross and refine our gold. This chapter helps us confess these flaws and to rest in the knowledge that God works all things together for those who love Him.

May 10, 2020

Sermon
"Daniel: Taming the Lion"
Daniel 6

CORPORATE PRAYER OF CONFESSION
AND ASSURANCE OF PARDON

Our Father, the apostle Paul writes, "Rejoice in hope, be patient in tribulation, be constant in prayer." We have to admit that we are failing on all three counts right now. This pandemic has us all bent out of shape. We confess to you that we haven't been doing a lot of rejoicing in recent weeks. Instead, we have filled our conversations with complaint. And as for patience, we have little of it. And instead of using this season to pray, some of us have spent too much of it frittering away the time on useless things. Forgive us, dear Lord. We are weak and fragile Christians at best. Reassure us again with gospel grace. Wash us clean again and help us to stand in your presence in full assurance and say with faith, "What a joy it is to be a Christian!" Amen.

(based on Romans 12:12)

Sermon
"The Free Exercise of Religion: Peter's First Amendment Moment"
Acts 4:1-22

CORPORATE PRAYER OF CONFESSION
AND ASSURANCE OF PARDON

Heavenly Father, James tells us, "Let every person be quick to hear, slow to speak, slow to anger." This COVID-19 season has all of us violating these commands. We are ready to voice our opinion, whether people want to listen or not. And as for listening, we are not sure to whom we should be listening to. And we have been angry and frustrated and often with those whom we love the most. Teach us a gentleness of spirit. Grant us the patience to think of others as better than ourselves. And, even when what we hear seems nonsense to us, grant us the grace to smile and be courteous. Thank you for the assurance that in Jesus, we are forgiven, totally and absolutely. Amen.

(based on James 1:19)

August 9, 2020

Sermon
"The Best Is Yet to Be"
Haggai 2:6-9

CORPORATE PRAYER OF CONFESSION

Father, we thank you that you are the God of peace. You have reconciled us to yourself through the gift of your Son. We love that verse which says, "being justified by faith we have peace with God." However, we confess that we have not always experienced that peace as we should. This season has made some of us irritable and angry. We are frustrated by almost every aspect of this season to the point of exasperation. And too often, we have taken it out on those we love the most. Forgive us, O Lord. Amen.

(based on II Thessalonians 3:16)

ASSURANCE OF PARDON

He will again have compassion on us;
   he will tread our iniquities underfoot.
You will cast all our sins
   into the depths of the sea.

(Micah 7:19)

October 25, 2020

Sermon
"Dirty Feet and Pride"
John 13:1-17

CORPORATE PRAYER OF CONFESSION

Heavenly Father, we read in Philippians the words of Paul concerning himself: "I can do all things through him who strengthens me." We think of him in prison in Rome facing a trial and possible execution. But he was calm and resolute. Father, we aren't in these circumstances, but we have to confess that we have not always been calm and resolute. We have been angry. We have snapped at those we love. We have been distrustful of your providence. We have felt sorry for ourselves and wallowed in self-pity. We have said things and done things that are unworthy, and we ask for your forgiveness today. Strengthen us today by the mighty power of the Holy Spirit. Remind us of our union and communion with Jesus. In Jesus' name. Amen.

(based on Philippians 4:13)

ASSURANCE OF PARDON

He will again have compassion on us;
    he will tread our iniquities underfoot.
You will cast all our sins
    into the depths of the sea.

(Micah 7:19)

Sermon
"Legalism 2"
Colossians 2:20-23

CORPORATE PRAYER OF CONFESSION

Heavenly Father, we confess that we find waiting difficult. Peter tells us you are not slow to fulfill your promise as some count slowness, but it often feels like an eternity to us. True, Peter was thinking about the Second Coming, but we find the same to be true about our personal lives. We want things to happen right now, and we get frustrated, or angry, or sad when they are delayed. Your ways are not our ways, and we ask forgiveness when we forget this important principle. Grant us patience to rest in the knowledge that you know best. In Jesus' name. Amen.

(based on II Peter 3:9)

ASSURANCE OF PARDON

For God so loved the world, that he gave his only Son, that whoever believes in him should not perish but have eternal life. For God did not send his Son into the world to condemn the world, but in order that the world might be saved through him.

(John 3:16-17)

November 15, 2020

Sermon
"Gone Fishing"
John 21:1-19

CORPORATE PRAYER OF CONFESSION

Heavenly Father, there is a trial in our life in this season, and we have been restless and complaining. We are truly sorry. This trial has been like a thorn in the flesh, a messenger of Satan. We have prayed that you would remove it, but it is still there. It is to keep us from conceit. Help us to listen to your voice saying, "My grace is sufficient for you, for my power is made perfect in weakness."

(based on II Corinthians 12:7-9)

ASSURANCE OF PARDON

Who is a God like you, pardoning iniquity
and passing over transgression
for the remnant of his inheritance?
He does not retain his anger forever,
because he delights in steadfast love.

(Micah 7:18)

Chapter 8
Confessions of Impure Thoughts

Paul exhorts us to think about things that are true, honorable, just, pure, lovely, commendable, excellent, and worthy of praise. We think about these things—sometimes. But not all the time. In fact, if we are honest, we think about these things only rarely and fleetingly. Instead, we dwell on our struggles, frustrations, anger, lusts, and bitterness. The confessions in this chapter help give voice to such sin, as the assurances exhort us to turn our thoughts toward the things that please God.

Sermon
"Rehoboam"
II Chronicles 10:1-19

CORPORATE PRAYER OF CONFESSION
AND ASSURANCE OF PARDON

Jesus said, "For out of the heart come evil thoughts, murder, adultery, sexual immorality, theft, false witness, slander." Our hearts are like a cesspool, full of the most terrible things. If our thoughts were to be projected onto a big screen for all to see, we would hide ourselves from the shame of it all. We want to do good, but evil is always present. Sometimes, these thoughts seem to come from "out of the blue"—fiery darts of the Evil One. Help us to resist him. Make him flee from us. Fill us with your Holy Spirit so that we may dwell on "whatever is true, whatever is honorable, whatever is just, whatever is pure, whatever is lovely, whatever is commendable." Thank you that in Jesus Christ there is forgiveness—complete and lasting forgiveness. Amen.

(based on Matthew 15:19 and Philippians 4:8)

November 8, 2020

Sermon
"The Accuser Meets with the Advocate"
Mark 14:66-72

CORPORATE PRAYER OF CONFESSION

Heavenly Father, we are responsible for what we think and the habit of thinking. We are exhorted in Philippians to "think about ... whatever is true, whatever is honorable, whatever is just, whatever is pure, whatever is lovely, whatever is commendable, ... and ... anything worthy of praise." We are what we think, and too often our thoughts betray the fact that we sin constantly in our heads. We would be totally ashamed to admit to some of our thoughts, but you know them all. And we ask forgiveness today. Cleanse our thoughts by the power of the Holy Spirit. In Jesus' name. Amen.

(based on Philippians 4:8-9)

ASSURANCE OF PARDON

"Come now, let us reason together, says the Lord:
though your sins are like scarlet,
    they shall be as white as snow;
though they are red like crimson,
    they shall become like wool."

(Isaiah 1:18)

April 11, 2021

Sermon
"The Penitential Psalm"
Psalm 51

CORPORATE PRAYER OF CONFESSION

Heavenly Father, we confess to you that our thoughts are never pure. In our imaginings, we transgress the boundaries of purity. Cleanse our minds that we may think your thoughts after you. As we journey continuously toward the celestial city, grant us a renewing of our minds, for you have promised that you will keep us in perfect peace whose mind is stayed on you. Let the Word of Christ dwell in us richly. We pray in Jesus' name. Amen.

ASSURANCE OF PARDON

Therefore, since we have been justified by faith, we have peace with God through our Lord Jesus Christ.

(Romans 5:1)

Chapter 9
Confessions of Pride

We are called to boast in the Lord and in our weakness, so that the power of Christ may shine through us. We constantly fall short. Rather than boasting in our Savior, we take pride in ourselves: our riches, successes, power, prestige, looks, possessions, connections, education, and accolades. None of those things can save us. And, compared to the good news of the gospel, all of the things in which we take pride are rubbish. God opposes the proud, James tells us, and these confessions help us to acknowledge this sin.

March 1, 2020

Sermon
"Cain"
Genesis 4:1-16

CORPORATE PRAYER OF CONFESSION
AND ASSURANCE OF PARDON

Heavenly Father, the Scriptures exhort us to confess our sins to each other and pray for each other so that we may be healed. We know all too well that when we sin, we often hurt other people and relationships sour. We feel as though a sickness exists in our souls. If such a situation comes to our minds right now, give us the grace and courage to say "sorry" and ask for forgiveness. Help us not to be too proud to do the right thing. Father, we pray for those we may have offended that you would bless them and fill their lives with a sense of your sweet presence. Prayers like this, your Word says, coming from a gospel-shaped heart, will be effective. That is because you are a kind and gracious God whose promises are "yes" and "Amen" in Jesus Christ. Amen.

(based on James 5:16)

September 6, 2020

Sermon
"A New Name"
John 1:35-42

CORPORATE PRAYER OF CONFESSION

Heavenly Father, your Word exhorts us to "continue steadfast in prayer, being watchful in it, with thanksgiving." We are always lamenting how little we pray. The very exhortation humbles us. Forgive us for our prayerlessness, signaling how little we trust you and how easily we slip into an autonomous stance trusting in our own strength and wisdom. We are so foolish. Help us to gain a renewed sense of the power of prayer this week. For Jesus' sake. Amen.

(based on Colossians 4:2)

ASSURANCE OF PARDON

Blessed be the God and Father of our Lord Jesus Christ! According to his great mercy, he has caused us to be born again to a living hope through the resurrection of Jesus Christ from the dead, to an inheritance that is imperishable, undefiled, and unfading, kept in heaven for you...

(I Peter 1:3-4)

September 13, 2020

Sermon
"A Sinful Man"
Luke 5:1-11

CORPORATE PRAYER OF CONFESSION

Heavenly Father, you told Paul to urge Euodia and Syntyche to "agree in the Lord." We don't know what these two women were disagreeing about, but it was obviously something trivial, else you would have told one of them to hold their ground. We can imagine what it might have been because we have quarreled with friends and loved ones, spouses and siblings, over trivial things. We have held grudges and held on to them for far too long. Some of us know what it is to lose a friendship or the trust of a relative because of stubborn hearts and a petulant nature. Forgive us for not humbling ourselves, thinking others better than ourselves. Wash us and cleanse us again in the blood of Christ. Help us reach out this week and, if needed, say sorry and mend these relationships. In Jesus' name. Amen.

(based on Philippians 4:2)

ASSURANCE OF PARDON

If we confess our sins, he is faithful and just to forgive us our sins and to cleanse us from all unrighteousness.

(I John 1:9)

Sermon
"Crab Is on the Menu"
Acts 10:1-48

CORPORATE PRAYER OF CONFESSION

Heavenly Father, I need your grace to be humble and contrite in the face of trials. I too often forget that it is in my weakness that your power is displayed. I sometimes behave like an angry toddler, throwing tantrums because things have not turned out as I expected. Calm my troubled heart. Pacify my volcanic outbursts. Help me to trust you in the outworking of your providence. For Jesus' sake. Amen.

(based on II Corinthians 12:9)

ASSURANCE OF PARDON

My sins, my sins, my Savior! They take such hold on me,
I am not able to look up, save only, Christ, to thee;
In thee is all forgiveness, in thee abundant grace,
My shadow and my sunshine the brightness of thy face.

(John S. B. Monsell, "My Sins, My Sins, My Savior!", stanza 1)

February 14, 2021

Sermon
"National Defeat"
Psalm 44

CORPORATE PRAYER OF CONFESSION

Almighty God, where can we go from your Spirit? Where can we flee from your presence? If we ascend into heaven, you are there! If we make our bed with the dead, you are there! If we dwell in the deepest part of the sea, you are there! Darkness and light are alike to you. You saw us before we were born, and we are written in your book all our days. There is nothing hidden from you.

What great comfort this is! But it is also humbling. We can fool others (and we so often do); we sometimes think that we can fool ourselves. But we can never fool you. Your omnipresence means you are closer to our sin than we desire to admit. And today we confess our "secret" sins to you and ask, again, in your tender mercy, for forgiveness in the blood of Christ, our Savior and Lord. Amen.

(based on Psalm 139)

ASSURANCE OF PARDON

If we confess our sins, he is faithful and just to forgive us our sins and to cleanse us from all unrighteousness.

(I John 1:9)

December 12, 2021

Sermon
"Thou Who Wast Rich Beyond All Splendor"
Philippians 2:5-11

CORPORATE PRAYER OF CONFESSION

Augustine suggested that pride was the very essence of sin, and we struggle with it all the time. We want to have our own way; we want to be in the limelight and be recognized, and our feelings get hurt when someone is recognized, and we are not. Help us to repent of this sin and be more Jesus-like who, being in the form of God, thought it not robbery to be equally with God, but emptied Himself. He made Himself nothing. He took the form of a servant. Help us be better at serving others. For Jesus' sake. Amen.

ASSURANCE OF PARDON

But when the fullness of time had come, God sent forth his Son, born of woman, born under the law, to redeem those who were under the law, so that we might receive adoption as sons. And because you are sons, God has sent the Spirit of his Son into our hearts, crying, "Abba! Father!" So you are no longer a slave, but a son, and if a son, then an heir through God.

(Galatians 4:4-7)

May 1, 2022

Sermon
"I Pray for... Those You Have Given Me"
John 17:6-10

CORPORATE PRAYER OF CONFESSION

Sin has a way of deceiving us. We are easily tempted through the exploitation of our weaknesses and strengths. We manipulate a narrative that convinces us that to sin in these circumstances, while wrong for others, is right for us. Too often we fall into sin because we did not allow ourselves time to think about what we were doing. We switched off our minds and conscience and ran headlong into sin. So teach us today to encourage one another, as long as it is called "today," so that none of us may be hardened by sin's deceitfulness. Amen.

(based on Hebrews 3:13)

ASSURANCE OF PARDON

Blessed be the LORD!
  For he has heard the voice of my pleas for mercy.
The LORD is my strength and my shield;
  in him my heart trusts, and I am helped;
my heart exults,
  and with my song I give thanks to him.

(Psalm 28:6-7)

September 25, 2022

Sermon
"Christ: The Head of the Body"
Colossians 1:18

CORPORATE PRAYER OF CONFESSION

Heavenly Father, Solomon tells us that, "When pride comes, then comes disgrace, but with the humble is wisdom." Pride, one theologian has said, is the very essence of sin. Pride is the boast that suggests we are more important than others, more important than you, O Lord. Our ego is too often exalted and, unlike the spirit of John the Baptist, we too often say, "He must decrease, but I must increase." Like hot-air balloons, we exalt ourselves too much. Forgive us, O Lord. Allow grace to puncture this pride and let out the conceit. Help us to shrink in deference to your honor and glory. Help us be at peace with the thought that we are servants, to be used by you in whatever way you please. In Jesus' name. Amen.

(based on Proverbs 11:2)

ASSURANCE OF PARDON

The LORD is merciful and gracious,
  slow to anger and abounding in steadfast love.
He will not always chide,
  nor will he keep his anger forever.
He does not deal with us according to our sins,
  nor repay us according to our iniquities.
For as high as the heavens are above the earth,
  so great is his steadfast love toward those who fear him;
as far as the east is from the west,
  so far does he remove our transgressions from us.

(Psalm 103:8-12)

April 2, 2023

Sermon
"The Triumphal Entry"
John 12:12-19

CORPORATE PRAYER OF CONFESSION

Heavenly Father, you have called us to walk in wisdom, "not as unwise but as wise." That means we walk in union with Christ, "the wisdom of God," and His written Word which "is able to make us wise." Forgive us that we often think and behave like fools, arrogantly putting our own thoughts and opinions ahead of yours. Help us not be like those of whom Jeremiah wrote, "[they] have neither listened nor inclined [their] ears to hear." In Jesus' name. Amen.

(based on Ephesians 5:15; I Corinthians 1:24;
II Timothy 3:15; and Jeremiah 25:4 and 44:5)

ASSURANCE OF PARDON

"Come now, let us reason together, says the LORD:
though your sins are like scarlet,
 they shall be as white as snow;
though they are red like crimson,
 they shall become like wool."

(Isaiah 1:18)

May 17, 2020

Sermon
"Jonah: Finding God in Unprecedented Circumstances"
Jonah 2

CORPORATE PRAYER OF CONFESSION
AND ASSURANCE OF PARDON

Heavenly Father, your Word commands us to "bear one another's burdens" for in doing so we "fulfill the law of Christ." Too often, we find ourselves wanting to focus on ourselves rather than others. We have problems, too, and sometimes we just want to wallow in self-pity. Lord, you know how often we have had pity-parties in these last few weeks. We are truly sorry. Help us to look outside of ourselves, to reach out to our brothers and sisters and neighbors, and see how we can help them. Help us to pray for one another regularly. And grant us the joy of knowing that all our sins are covered by the blood of Jesus. Amen.

(based on Galatians 6:2-5)

October 23, 2022

Sermon
"Christ in You, the Hope of Glory"
Colossians 1:24-27

CORPORATE PRAYER OF CONFESSION

Heavenly Father, you tell us to "bear one another's burdens, and so fulfill the law of Christ." This is one of the good works that you have planned for us. This will please you. It is our family code. Forgive us for our selfishness, considering our own trials more important than our neighbor's. Forgive us when we fail to be Christlike in responding to the burdens of our brother or sister. Forgive us when we have shown too little empathy, too little love, and too few expressions of practical help. In Jesus' name. Amen.

(based on Galatians 6:2)

ASSURANCE OF PARDON

There is therefore now no condemnation for those who are in Christ Jesus.

(Romans 8:1)

January 29, 2023

Sermon
"Legalism 1"
Colossians 2:16-19

CORPORATE PRAYER OF CONFESSION

Heavenly Father, we have sinned against you in thought, word, and deed. And we are capable of far more had it not been for your restraining hand upon us. Our sins seem like an irrational rebellion against all that is good and noble, a lawless pattern of putting ourselves first and avoiding submission to your authority and guidance. Forgive us, O Lord, and grant us grace to turn from these wicked ways and follow you with all our heart. In Jesus' name. Amen.

ASSURANCE OF PARDON

Whoever conceals his transgressions will not prosper,
    but he who confesses and forsakes them will obtain mercy.

(Proverbs 28:13)

March 12, 2023

Sermon
"Putting On"
Colossians 3:12-14

CORPORATE PRAYER OF CONFESSION

Heavenly Father, in saving us, we are meant to become more and more like the Lord Jesus. We are meant to put on "compassionate hearts, kindness, humility, meekness, and patience" and to bear with one another, and forgive one another. Instead, we see too much lack of concern, thoughtlessness, pride, conceit, and irritability. We confess that these sins remain in our hearts. We have held on to wrongs committed against us, refusing to forgive when we have been forgiven by your great mercy. Have mercy on us, we pray. In Jesus' name. Amen.

(based on Colossians 3:12-14)

ASSURANCE OF PARDON

Pardon for sin and a peace that endureth
Thine own dear presence to cheer and to guide;
Strength for today and bright hope for tomorrow,
Blessings all mine, with ten thousand beside!

(Thomas O. Chisholm, "Great is Thy Faithfulness", stanza 3)

March 19, 2023

Sermon
"A New Song"
Colossians 3:15-17

CORPORATE PRAYER OF CONFESSION

Paul exhorts us this way: "Whatever you do, in word or deed, do everything in the name of the Lord Jesus, giving thanks to God the Father through him." This we have not consistently done. Too often, we do things simply for our own benefit. We have not always consulted you or sought your guidance and direction. And we most certainly have not always been thankful for your providence, resorting instead to complaining and feeling sorry for ourselves. Forgive us, O Lord our God. In Jesus' name. Amen.

(based on Colossians 3:17)

ASSURANCE OF PARDON

The Lord is merciful and gracious,
  slow to anger and abounding in steadfast love.
He will not always chide,
  nor will he keep his anger forever.
He does not deal with us according to our sins,
  nor repay us according to our iniquities.
For as high as the heavens are above the earth,
  so great is his steadfast love toward those who fear him;
as far as the east is from the west,
  so far does he remove our transgressions from us.

(Psalm 103:8-12)

April 16, 2023

Sermon
"Work"
Colossians 3:23-4:1

CORPORATE PRAYER OF CONFESSION

Heavenly Father, you placed Adam in the Garden of Eden and told him "to work it and keep it." There would have been no pain. There were no "thorns and thistles" to cause the work to fail and be burdensome. We labor in a fallen world. Our motives are often twisted and turned in upon ourselves. We become experts in excuses. We fail to focus and exert proper energy in fulfilling our obligations. Help us to fulfill Solomon's statement that there is "nothing better than that a man should rejoice in his work, for that is his lot."

(based on Genesis 2:15 and 3:18 and Ecclesiastes 3:22)

ASSURANCE OF PARDON

Blessed be the God and Father of our Lord Jesus Christ! According to his great mercy, he has caused us to be born again to a living hope through the resurrection of Jesus Christ from the dead, to an inheritance that is imperishable, undefiled, and unfading, kept in heaven for you...

(I Peter 1:3-4)

May 14, 2023

Sermon
"More Friends in Need"
Colossians 4:10-17

CORPORATE PRAYER OF CONFESSION

Heavenly Father, Scripture exhorts us to "encourage one another" and especially to "encourage the fainthearted, help the weak, be patient with them all." Too often we have failed to do that. We have failed to give a word of appreciation to those who have ministered to us. We have been so busy attending to our own needs that we have failed to comfort those who are in need. We are heartily sorry and ask for your forgiveness. In Jesus' name. Amen.

(based on I Thessalonians 5:14)

ASSURANCE OF PARDON

Who has believed what he has heard from us?
    And to whom has the arm of the LORD been revealed?
For he grew up before him like a young plant,
    and like a root out of dry ground;
he had no form or majesty that we should look at
    him, and no beauty that we should desire him.
He was despised and rejected by men,
    a man of sorrows and acquainted with grief;
and as one from whom men hide their faces
    he was despised, and we esteemed him not.

Surely he has borne our griefs
    and carried our sorrows;
yet we esteemed him stricken,
    smitten by God, and afflicted.
But he was pierced for our transgressions;
    he was crushed for our iniquities;
upon him was the chastisement that brought us
    peace, and with his wounds we are healed.

(Isaiah 53:1-5)

May 28, 2023

Sermon
"The Golden Chain"
Romans 8:28-29

CORPORATE PRAYER OF CONFESSION

Heavenly Father, our salvation depends upon a choice you made from before the foundation of the world. Our confidence of getting to heaven lies solely on your power and faithfulness. For this, we should be filled with gratitude and praise. But we confess that, too often, we fail to thank you. We are too preoccupied with ourselves and our needs to properly express how much we owe you—a debt we can never repay. Forgive us, O Lord. In Jesus' name. Amen.

ASSURANCE OF PARDON

For the wages of sin is death, but the free gift of God is eternal life in Christ Jesus our Lord.

(Romans 6:23)

Chapter 10
Confessions of Shame

When we see our sin for how wretched it really is, we grieve and hate it. Yet sometimes we allow the shame we feel over our sin to overwhelm us. In these moments, we must remember that Jesus' blood is sufficient to atone for all our sins.

January 19, 2020

Sermon
"The Cross"
John 19:16b-37

CORPORATE PRAYER OF CONFESSION
AND ASSURANCE OF PARDON

Lord, we have sinned against you so many times without number. We are ashamed to lift up our face before you. With the psalmist, we say, "For my iniquities have gone over my head; like a heavy burden, they are too heavy for me." If you, O Lord should mark iniquity, O Lord, who could stand? How shall we answer you? We lay our hands upon our mouths. We have no answer to your righteous indignation. But you do. You have provided a substitute, your own dear Son, our Savior Jesus Christ. All we like sheep have gone astray, but you have laid on Him the iniquity of us all. Amen.

(based on Psalm 23 and Psalm 38)

Sermon
"The Strange Twists of the Christian Life"
I Peter 1:1-9

CORPORATE PRAYER OF CONFESSION

Gracious and most merciful Father, we come again confessing our sins, knowing as we do so, that you are rich in mercy and abounding in steadfast love. We are spiritually poor, but you are full of grace and truth. You have made a covenant that promises pardon to those who cast themselves into the arms of your Son and our Savior Jesus Christ. We are ashamed that, in union with Him, we still listen to the voice of the enemy, continue to sin in thought, word, and deed. We are too often weak in faith, and so we ask you to strengthen us by the power of the Holy Spirit. We are too often cold in our reciprocal love, and so we ask you to renew us from the inside out. Hear us, O Lord. In Jesus' name. Amen.

ASSURANCE OF PARDON

It will be said on that day,
    "Behold, this is our God; we have waited for him, that he might save us.
    This is the LORD; we have waited for him;
    let us be glad and rejoice in his salvation."

(Isaiah 25:9)

Chapter 11
Confessions of Unwholesome Talk

The apostle James wrote that "no human being can tame the tongue" when he explained the harm that such a small part of our body can wreak. Sadly, our lives have proven this point time and again. We must confess how our speech does not reflect the grace of God, the love of Christ, or the power of the Spirit.

August 30, 2020

Sermon
"When God Says, 'I Will'"
Haggai 2:20-23

CORPORATE PRAYER OF CONFESSION

Heavenly Father, your Word tells us, "Let no corrupting talk come out of your mouths, but only such as is good for building up, as fits the occasion, that it may give grace to those who hear." We are surprised by the unwholesome words that come out of our mouths. Words that bear terrible realities that we employ in trivializing ways as in the use of your holy name, or "heaven" or "hell." And then there are the words we use when speaking of others, friends and foes. Unwholesome, mean-spirited, character-assassinating words that fail to show respect and common courtesy. Forgive us, O Lord, and help us to use our tongue in a Christlike manner. For Jesus' sake. Amen.

(based on Ephesians 4:29)

ASSURANCE OF PARDON

Pardon for sin and a peace that endureth,
Thine own dear presence to cheer and to guide;
Strength for today and bright hope for tomorrow,
Blessings all mine, with ten thousand beside!
Great is Thy faithfulness! Great is Thy faithfulness!
Morning by morning new mercies I see;
All I have needed Thy hand hath provided—
Great is Thy faithfulness, Lord, unto me!

(Thomas O. Chisholm, "Great is Thy Faithfulness", stanza 3)

January 24, 2021

Sermon
"Rescued by an Angel"
Acts 12:6-19

CORPORATE PRAYER OF CONFESSION

Heavenly Father, your Word is very clear: the powers that be are ordained of God. To resist them, willfully, is to resist you. In the turbulence of our nation this week, we ask for grace to demonstrate a Christian mindset in all that we do, particularly as we relate to our fellow brothers and sisters with whom we may disagree on political matters. Today we want to confess that too often sin enters when we read the news, offer our opinions on social media, express our thoughts to others. Grant us the grace of Christian humility and especially the grace to be like Jesus, who described Himself as "gentle." For Jesus' sake. Amen.

(based on Romans 13:1-2)

ASSURANCE OF PARDON

Pardon for sin and a peace that endureth,
Thine own dear presence to cheer and to guide;
Strength for today and bright hope for tomorrow,
Blessings all mine, with ten thousand beside!
Great is Thy faithfulness! Great is Thy faithfulness!
Morning by morning new mercies I see;
All I have needed Thy hand hath provided—
Great is Thy faithfulness, Lord, unto me!

(Thomas O. Chisholm, *Great is Thy Faithfulness*, stanza 3)

February 28, 2021

Sermon
"Unshakeable City"
Psalm 46

CORPORATE PRAYER OF CONFESSION

Heavenly Father, this morning we recall Paul's words to the church in Rome, "We who are strong have an obligation to bear with the failings of the weak, and not to please ourselves." We confess that we are often irritated and intolerant of those who disagree with us about matters that are not essential to the faith. We fail to "build up" our neighbors and instead tread all over them and, in doing so, fail to follow the example of our Savior who "did not please himself." Forgive us for the sins of arrogance and pride. Forgive us for treating one another with disdain. Grant us the grace to emulate more and more the mindset of Jesus. Amen.

(based on Romans 15:1-2)

ASSURANCE OF PARDON

To the Lord our God belong mercy and forgiveness...

(Daniel 9:9)

Chapter 12
Confessions for Special Occasions

We should confess our sins daily. But experience teaches us that some occasions tend to make us reflect more deeply upon our sins. This chapter includes confessions for some of these moments, including the Lord's Supper and Christmas.

January 12, 2020

Sermon
"Truth or Fiction"
John 18:28-40

COMMUNION PRAYER BASED ON
THE TEN COMMANDMENTS

Father, Son and Holy Spirit, we adore you and love you.

We confess you to be the only God there is, and we revere you.
Help us to tear down idols we create in our hearts that hide you from us.
Enable us to speak of you with reverence and awe.
Make the Lord's Day special to us.
Thank you for our parents, for their love and sacrifice.
Have mercy on our land for the slaying of the unborn.
Keep our intimate lives pure and holy.
Grant us integrity in matters of property and time.
Forgive us for lies, big or small.
Fill us with contentment in the provisions of your providence.

Wash us and cleanse us in the blood of Christ, for Jesus' sake. Amen.

December 5, 2021

Sermon
"Of the Father's Love Begotten"
John 1:14

CORPORATE PRAYER OF CONFESSION

As we enter Advent season, we are reminded of the reason for the incarnation of Christ into the world—to save sinners like us. Without His sacrificial, substitutionary death on our behalf, we would still be in our sins and facing an eternity of torment. Even now, though we have been Christians for many years, we find to our dismay that we keep on sinning against you. We are truly sorry and come to you in a spirit of repentance to ask for forgiveness once again. We need Christmas and Easter before us every day. Hear us, O Lord, in Jesus' name. Amen.

ASSURANCE OF PARDON

If we confess our sins, he is faithful and just to forgive us our sins and to cleanse us from all unrighteousness.

(1 John 1:9)

December 3, 2023

Sermon
"The Birth of Jesus Christ"
Matthew 1:18-25

CORPORATE PRAYER OF CONFESSION

Heavenly Father, it is Christmas season again and we come to you asking forgiveness for not contemplating its necessity the way we ought. We think of Jesus lying in the manger, and shepherds on Bethlehem's hillsides, and choirs of angels, but we forget that Jesus came to save us from our sins. He veiled His glory and became a servant as our sin-bearer and substitute. Forgive us for making too light of sin, *our* sin. And forgive us, too, for neglecting to contemplate the wonder of your love for us in sending your Son into this fallen world to redeem us. In Jesus' name. Amen.

(based on Matthew 1:18-25)

ASSURANCE OF PARDON

Comfort, comfort my people, says your God.
Speak tenderly to Jerusalem,
   and cry to her
that her warfare is ended,
   that her iniquity is pardoned,
that she has received from the LORD's hand
   double for all her sins.

(Isaiah 40:1-2)

December 10, 2023

Sermon
"The Shepherds and the Angels"
Luke 1:8-21

CORPORATE PRAYER OF CONFESSION

Heavenly Father, we ask forgiveness today for not always feeling the "great joy" that the first Christmas promised. You sent your only begotten Son into this world to lie in a manger so that, through faith in His finished work on our behalf, our sins might be forgiven, and that we may have peace with you. Pardon us when we fail to appreciate the glory of what has been achieved for us. Forgive us when there is no song in our hearts. In Jesus' name. Amen.

(based on Luke 2:8-21)

ASSURANCE OF PARDON

This is the message we have heard from him and proclaim to you, that God is light, and in him is no darkness at all. If we say we have fellowship with him while we walk in darkness, we lie and do not practice the truth. But if we walk in the light, as he is in the light, we have fellowship with one another, and the blood of Jesus his Son cleanses us from all sin.

(1 John 1:5-7)

December 19, 2021

Sermon
"What Child Is This?"
I John 1:1-4

CORPORATE PRAYER OF CONFESSION

This is the most wonderful time of the year when we get to think again about the birth of our Savior. Forgive us that we too easily get caught up in all the festivities and forget that it is supposed to be all about Jesus. Forgive us when busy-ness becomes an idol. Help us to have moments in the week ahead when we can stop and take in the sheer wonder of it all—that the second person of the Trinity took on human flesh and blood and was found lying in a manger. We ask this in Jesus' name. Amen.

ASSURANCE OF PARDON

God shows his love for us in that while we were still
sinners, Christ died for us.
Arise, shine, for his light has come,
and the glory of the Lord has risen upon you.

(Romans 5:8 and Isaiah 60:1)

December 17, 2023

Sermon
"The Visit of the Wise Men"
Matthew 2:1-12

CORPORATE PRAYER OF CONFESSION

Heavenly Father, wise men followed Jesus, and they still do. Forgive us for times of folly when we have failed to humble ourselves, failed to be joyful, failed to do your will, and failed to have that peace that passes all understanding. Grant us grace that will bind us to yourself, every day and in every way, a wisdom that makes us faithful to you. For Jesus' sake. Amen.

(based on Matthew 2:1-12)

ASSURANCE OF PARDON

No more let sins and sorrows grow,
Nor thorns infest the ground;
He comes to make His blessings flow
Far as the curse is found.

From the Christmas Carol, "Joy to the World! The Lord is Come"

December 18, 2022

Sermon
"In the Eye of an Eagle"
John 1:1-14

CORPORATE PRAYER OF CONFESSION

Heavenly Father, we thank you for sending your Son, the light of the world, to Bethlehem for us. Too often we live as though darkness continues to prevail. We blot out the brightness of His face that shines upon us every day. We forget that the light continues to shine brightly. Forgive us for walking in the shadows. As Advent approaches, aid us by your Holy Spirit to walk as "children of light, children of the day." For Jesus' sake. Amen.

(based on Matthew 5:14; I Thessalonians 5:5; and John 1:7 and 8:12)

ASSURANCE OF PARDON

But when the fullness of time had come, God sent forth his Son, born of woman, born under the law, to redeem those who were under the law, so that we might receive adoption as sons. And because you are sons, God has sent the Spirit of his Son into our hearts, crying, "Abba! Father!" So you are no longer a slave, but a son, and if a son, then an heir through God.

(Galatians 4:4-7)

December 24, 2023

Sermon
"The Word Made Flesh"
John 1:14

CORPORATE PRAYER OF CONFESSION

Heavenly Father, there have been too many times when we have worshiped in this place and failed to see the glory that shines in the face of Jesus Christ. We have gone through the motions of worship, repeating the Lord's Prayer and the Apostles' Creed, but we have failed to be moved by the blessings that are ours in Jesus Christ. Forgive us, O Lord! In Jesus' name. Amen.

ASSURANCE OF PARDON

For the wages of sin is death, but the free gift of God is eternal life in Christ Jesus our Lord.

(Romans 6:23)

December 25, 2022

Sermon
"In the Manger at Bethlehem"
Luke 2:1-7

CORPORATE PRAYER OF CONFESSION

Joy was your plan for us from the very beginning and today, Christmas Day, is a testament to it. The angel's words to fearful shepherds reminded them of it: "Fear not, for behold, I bring you good news of great joy that will be for all the people." Forgive us for not being joyful, even in our sorrows. Remind us of the "inexpressible gift" that is Jesus Christ. Amen.

(based on Luke 2:10 and II Corinthians 9:15)

ASSURANCE OF PARDON

Therefore, since we have been justified by faith, we have peace with God through our Lord Jesus Christ.

(Romans 5:1)

Chapter 13
Confessions from II Timothy

Dr. Thomas's last sermon series as the Senior Minister at First Presbyterian Church was II Timothy. This epistle was Paul's last set of instructions to Timothy before Paul was executed by the Roman authorities. These are the confessions and assurances Dr. Thomas used during his final season in the pulpit in Columbia, South Carolina.

August 13, 2023

Sermon
"Alive in Christ"
II Timothy 1:1-2

CORPORATE CONFESSION OF SIN

Heavenly Father, you have made us to be alive in Christ. We were once dead in trespasses and sins, but you quickened us by the power of the Holy Spirit. Forgive us for not reckoning on this every moment of our lives. Forgive us for living as though we were still in Adam rather than in Christ. Forgive us for not being thankful to you for all that you have done and have promised to do in us and through us and for us. In Jesus' name. Amen.

(based on Romans 6:11; Ephesians 2:1, 5; and II Timothy 1:1)

ASSURANCE OF PARDON

The LORD is merciful and gracious,
   slow to anger and abounding in steadfast love.
He will not always chide,
   nor will he keep his anger forever.
He does not deal with us according to our sins,
   nor repay us according to our iniquities.
For as high as the heavens are above the earth,
   so great is his steadfast love toward those who fear him;
as far as the east is from the west,
   so far does he remove our transgressions from us.

(Psalm 103:8-12)

August 20, 2023

Sermon
"A Gospel Family"
II Timothy 1:3-7

CORPORATE PRAYER OF CONFESSION

Heavenly Father, we are prone to forget that the Holy Spirit is a Spirit of power. In our sloth we simply go through the motions, but our heart is not on fire as it should be. We are turned in upon ourselves and are too timid. We are only half invested, and the embers of our love for you are almost extinguished. Forgive us, O Lord. Light a fire within us today so that we demonstrate the life of Christ in all our words and actions. In Jesus' Name. Amen.

(based on II Timothy 1:7)

ASSURANCE OF PARDON

There is a fountain filled with blood,
Drawn from Immanuel's veins;
And sinners, plunged beneath that flood,
Lose all their guilty stains.

(William Cowper, "There Is a Fountain Filled with Blood", stanza 1)

August 27, 2023

Sermon
"Prison Time"
II Timothy 1:8-12

CORPORATE PRAYER OF CONFESSION

We confess, O Lord, that we would prefer our lives to be filled with comfort rather than pressure, rewards rather than sacrifice, tranquility rather than suffering. But you have told us that if we wish to follow Jesus, we must be prepared to die to ourselves and face the hatred of an unbelieving world and the spite of Satan. Forgive us our sins we pray, in Jesus' name. Amen.

(based on II Timothy 1:8 and Matthew 16:24-26)

ASSURANCE OF PARDON

"Seek the LORD while he may be found;
    call upon him while he is near;
let the wicked forsake his way,
    and the unrighteous man his thoughts;
let him return to the LORD, that he may have compassion on him,
    and to our God, for he will abundantly pardon."

(Isaiah 55:6-7)

September 3, 2023

Sermon
"The Pattern of Sound Words"
II Timothy 1:13-18

CORPORATE PRAYER OF CONFESSION

Heavenly Father, your Word tells that we are to "follow the pattern of the sound words that you have heard." We live in a society where there are few sound words, and we need your help to keep us faithful to what you have taught us in Scripture. Forgive us when we give way to cultural worldviews that are at odds with Scripture. Grant us winsomeness in defending "the faith that was once for all delivered to the saints." In Jesus' name. Amen.

(based on II Timothy 1:13 and Jude 3)

ASSURANCE OF PARDON

"For this is the covenant that I will make with the
house of Israel after those days, declares the Lord:
I will put my laws into their minds,
    and write them on their hearts,
and I will be their God,
    and they shall be my people.
For I will be merciful toward their iniquities,
    and I will remember their sins no more."

(Hebrews 8:10, 12)

September 17, 2023

Sermon
"Trustworthy Saying"
II Timothy 2:8-13

CORPORATE PRAYER OF CONFESSION

Heavenly Father, we are "prone to wander, Lord, I feel it; prone to leave the God I love." Our text today reminds us that we need to endure, to persevere in the face of every trial and obstacle. There are temptations that might cause us to deny you, situations where we are disposed to be faithless. Forgive us when we have failed to be alert, when our hearts have been cold, when our zeal has subsided. Come, Holy Spirit, and renew us. In Jesus' name. Amen.

(based on II Timothy 2:12-13 and Robert Robinson, "Come, Thou Fount of Every Blessing")

ASSURANCE OF PARDON

Who is a God like you, pardoning iniquity
   and passing over transgression
   for the remnant of his inheritance?
He does not retain his anger forever,
   because he delights in steadfast love.
He will again have compassion on us;
   he will tread our iniquities underfoot.
You will cast all our sins
   into the depths of the sea.

(Micah 7:18-19)

September 24, 2023

Sermon
"Sound Preaching"
II Timothy 2:14-21

CORPORATE PRAYER OF CONFESSION

Heavenly Father, the apostle Paul counsels Timothy to "avoid irreverent babble" because it leads to "more and more ungodliness." We have had our share of irreverent talk, words spoken in haste, leading to spiritual gangrene, a decay of the soul. Forgive us, O Lord. Enable our words to be "seasoned with salt." For Jesus' sake. Amen.

(based on II Timothy 2:16 and Colossians 4:6)

ASSURANCE OF PARDON

For while we were still weak, at the right time Christ died for the ungodly. For one will scarcely die for a righteous person—though perhaps for a good person one would dare even to die—but God shows his love for us in that while we were still sinners, Christ died for us.

(Romans 5:6-8)

October 1, 2023

Sermon
"The Qualities of a Good Preacher"
II Timothy 2:22-26

CORPORATE PRAYER OF CONFESSION

Heavenly Father, we are the body of Christ, the people of God, the bride of Christ. You have brought us together as the family of God. Some of us have been quarrelsome and sometimes lacking in kindness and patience. Forgive us, O Lord, in Jesus' name. Amen.

(based on II Timothy 2:24)

ASSURANCE OF PARDON

It will be said on that day,
"Behold, this is our God; we have waited for him,
that he might save us.
This is the LORD; we have waited for him;
let us be glad and rejoice in his salvation."

(Isaiah 25:9)

October 8, 2023

Sermon
"People to Avoid"
II Timothy 3:1-9

CORPORATE PRAYER OF CONFESSION

Heavenly Father, too often we pretend to worship but our hearts are cold and distant. We "have the appearance of godliness," but not its "power." We flirt with outward Christianity as though you cannot fully read our hearts. Help us this morning by the power of the Holy Spirit to worship you "in spirit and in truth." For Jesus' sake. Amen.

(based on II Timothy 3:5 and John 4:24)

ASSURANCE OF PARDON

The LORD passed before him and proclaimed, "The LORD, the LORD, a God merciful and gracious, slow to anger, and abounding in steadfast love and faithfulness, keeping steadfast love for thousands, forgiving iniquity and transgression and sin."

There is therefore now no condemnation for those who are in Christ Jesus.

(Exodus 34:6-7a and Romans 8:1)

October 15, 2023

Sermon
"Persecution"
II Timothy 3:10-13

CORPORATE PRAYER OF CONFESSION

Paul reminds us that "all who desire to live a godly life will be persecuted."
We confess that we know little of persecution because we have conformed
too easily to the narrative of this world. We have not denied ourselves and
taken up a cross and followed Jesus as we should have done. We ask for your
forgiveness. Grant us the courage to stand winsomely apart from the world.
For Jesus' sake. Amen.

(based on II Timothy 3:12 and Matthew 16:24)

ASSURANCE OF PARDON

(Jesus said) "I am the living bread that came down from heaven. If anyone
eats of this bread, he will live forever."

(John 6:51)

October 22, 2023

Sermon
"The Sacred Writings"
II Timothy 3:16-17

CORPORATE PRAYER OF CONFESSION

"Your word is a lamp to my feet and a light to my path." The Bible is your good gift to us, to make us "wise for salvation through faith in Christ Jesus." Jesus said that "Scripture cannot be broken;" its statements are true, it cannot contradict itself. We confess that we have many copies of the Bible in our homes, but we spend too little time reading them. And even when we do, we fail to give you the glory. We are not always worshipful as we approach your Word. Too often, no song of praise has come from our lips as we hear your covenant promises to us. Renew in us today a love for the Scriptures. In Jesus' name. Amen.

(based on Psalm 119:105; II Timothy 3:15; and John 10:35)

ASSURANCE OF PARDON

The Lord is merciful and gracious,
  slow to anger and abounding in steadfast love.
He will not always chide,
  nor will he keep his anger forever.
He does not deal with us according to our sins,
  nor repay us according to our iniquities.
  For as high as the heavens are above the earth,
so great is his steadfast love toward those who fear him;
as far as the east is from the west,
  so far does he remove our transgressions from us.

(Psalm 103:8-12)

November 5, 2023

Sermon
"Sound Teaching"
II Timothy 4:1-4

CORPORATE PRAYER OF CONFESSION

We confess that our minds are often tickled by unsound preaching and teaching, offering easier paths to follow, and the allurement of treasures of an earthly sort to be acquired. We are easily tempted to cross over onto By-Path Meadow and regret it when we arrive in Doubting Castle and in the presence of Giant Despair. Grant us courage to follow the sound teaching of Scripture and not to flinch at the cost of it when it goes against the teachings of the world we live in. In Jesus' name. Amen.

(based on II Timothy 4:2-3 and John Bunyan, "Pilgrim's Progress")

ASSURANCE OF PARDON

For you know the grace of our Lord Jesus Christ, that though he was rich, yet for your sake he became poor, so that you by his poverty might become rich.

(II Corinthians 8:9)

November 26, 2023

Sermon
"Grace Be with You"
II Timothy 4:9-22

CORPORATE PRAYER OF CONFESSION

Heavenly Father, we confess that we are prone to leave you. The treachery of Demas should spur us on to follow you more closely. We also confess that we have not loved books that speak of you and your work in saving us as much as we ought. We have loved amusement more than searching out the hidden treasures of the gospel. Nor have we valued the grace that is revealed in Jesus as much as we ought. Forgive us, O Lord and cleanse us afresh in the atoning blood of Christ. In Jesus' name. Amen.

(based on II Timothy 4:9-22)

ASSURANCE OF PARDON

Though Satan should buffet, though trials should come,
Let this blest assurance control,
That Christ has regarded my helpless estate,
And hath shed His own blood for my soul.

My sin, oh, the bliss of this glorious thought!
My sin, not in part but the whole,
Is nailed to the cross, and I bear it no more,
Praise the Lord, praise the Lord, O my soul!

(Horatio G. Spafford, "It Is Well with My Soul", stanzas 2 and 3)

Afterword

A fellow pastor and I were once discussing the place of a prayer of confession in public worship. He was very pro-prayer of confession. He thought it a marvelous measure. At such a time, he said, it was as if the Lord's people could exclaim, "We get to repent!" I had to agree—and yet one may look in vain to find a prayer of confession lurking somewhere in many churches today. Actually, strange as it seems, one can look hard to find prayer at all. I've observed there can be nearly thirty minutes of singing under the jurisdiction of a praise band and a possible exposition of Scripture following, but, aside from a prayer-ditty at the beginning or close of the service, hardly any prayer at all, least of all prayers of confession or intercession. Strange, prayerless churches.

Someone has said that only the church confesses sins. That's probably true. After all, the Rotary Club doesn't confess sins, nor the local chapter of the PTA. The United States Senate doesn't stand and confess its iniquities, nor does a convention of pulmonary pathologists. No, only the church confesses sins. Sometimes.

That "sometimes" is because not all churches make a place for such in their worship. First Presbyterian, Columbia, does. That's both proper and problematical. Problematical, because there are fine prayers of confession we can use, but they have been used over and over to the point that we've become so accustomed to their content and cadence that we've become "tone deaf" to them and can easily slip into thoughtless, mechanical repetition. The familiar becomes deadening.

This is a danger with anything we do with regularity. How often have you perhaps exited your morning shower and the first action you take consists of applying your deodorant? You always do it that way. But a moment or two later as you gaze in the mirror and prepare to brush your teeth, you ask yourself, "Did I use deodorant?" You know you always do it but since it's such an ingrained habit, you don't know if you did it when you did it! You assume you did but have no conscious memory of it. So you reach for the deodorant stick and apply more. Even a few minutes later in the morning ritual, self-doubt can enter again: "Am I *sure* that I...?" That's why intense people with high anxiety have trouble with chafed underarms.

So...when it comes to our customary worship practices, like prayers of confession, we need someone to "run around end" of our mechanical tendencies, resurrect our attention, and come at these matters with freshness and variety. And that is where

Dr. Thomas has put us in his debt. In a multi-tasking way, he helps us see and confess our multi-faceted sin, anchoring such prayers on a plethora of different biblical texts. This keeps us from going from a practice to a groove to a rut in our efforts at public confession.

Now, however, that we have these prayers and assurances collected in one handy tome, it means we can use these public worship helps for personal and family worship. We can also note and meditate on the biblical texts Derek used as the basis for these prayers. And we can get out our hymnbook and sing a number of the assurances of pardon. In short, here is a devotional treasury plunked into our hands.

In one of his books, Warren Wiersbe passes on an anecdote about Alexander Whyte, the 19th and early 20th century minister of Free St. George's in Edinburgh. Whyte was known for his brutal, penetrating unmasking of sin. Once, two miners from the Highlands were visiting the city and worshiped at St. George's. Whyte's sermon that day had been a vintage expose of sin. The men left the church in deep silence. After a few blocks, one said to the other, "Sandy, yon man must have been a *deevil* when he was a laddie!" Well, how else would he know sin so well? After reading these prayers, one might be tempted to say the same about Derek! Until we realize that these prayers depict our own condition. Yet what good news they carry: "We get to repent!"

Dale Ralph Davis

Christian Focus Publications

Our mission statement

Staying Faithful

In dependence upon God we seek to impact the world through literature faithful to His infallible Word, the Bible. Our aim is to ensure that the Lord Jesus Christ is presented as the only hope to obtain forgiveness of sin, live a useful life and look forward to heaven with Him.

Our Books are published in four imprints:

◁◯✕ CHRISTIAN FOCUS

Popular works including biographies, commentaries, basic doctrine and Christian living.

◁◯✕ MENTOR

Books written at a level suitable for Bible College and seminary students, pastors, and other serious readers. The imprint includes commentaries, doctrinal studies, examination of current issues and church history.

◁◯✕ CHRISTIAN HERITAGE

Books representing some of the best material from the rich heritage of the church.

◁◯✕ CF4KIDS

Children's books for quality Bible teaching and for all age groups: Sunday school curriculum, puzzle and activity books; personal and family devotional titles, biographies and inspirational stories – because you are never too young to know Jesus!

Christian Focus Publications Ltd,
Geanies House, Fearn, Ross-shire,
IV20 1TW, Scotland, United Kingdom.
www.christianfocus.com